WRITING AS PUNISHMENT

WRITING AS PUNISHMENT IN SCHOOLS, COURTS, AND EVERYDAY LIFE

SPENCER SCHAFFNER

THE UNIVERSITY OF ALABAMA PRESS

TUSCALOOSA

The University of Alabama Press
Tuscaloosa, Alabama 35487-0380
uapress.ua.edu

Inquiries about reproducing material from this work should
be addressed to the University of Alabama Press.

Typeface: Scala Pro, Scala Sans Pro, and Avenir

Cover image: Detail from Hieronymus Bosch, *The Garden of
Earthly Delights* (1490–1500), Museo del Prado, Madrid

Cover design: David Nees

Cataloging-in-Publication data is available from the Library of Congress.
ISBN: 978-0-8173-2022-5 (cloth)
ISBN: 978-0-8173-5955-3 (paper)
E-ISBN: 978-0-8173-9236-9

For Phineas

CONTENTS

ACKNOWLEDGMENTS

This book began in the classroom, where, for over a decade, I have asked preservice teachers to consider why writing is used as punishment. Through those stimulating conversations, I was moved to write this book. Halfway through writing this manuscript, I faced some health issues that made writing a challenge. Thank you to Melissa Littlefield, for never once doubting this project. Thanks to my son, Phineas, for modeling what it means to be dedicated and passionate about so many things in life. Thanks to Zach, for describing how writing has been used as punishment in local schools. Thanks to my mother, Marie Schaffner, for always asking about the book, and to my sisters, Monica, Leah, and Jennifer, for unwavering support on all levels. Two friends, Lisa Nakamura and Debra Hawhee, offered useful citations and clever ways of framing the project at a critical moment. Thanks to Amy and Steve Cartwright for unwavering encouragement, often in the great outdoors. Before her untimely death, I was fortunate to correspond with Jennifer Kempton, who challenged me to think critically about writing and exploitation. Dan Waterman at the University of Alabama Press has been a joy to work with and extraordinarily helpful in moving this book through the publication processes, and I am humbled by the two anonymous reviewers who provided me with detailed readings of the manuscript, adding to the project in countless ways.

WRITING AS PUNISHMENT

INTRODUCTION

There is a fairly consistent and prevalent belief that writing and literacy are edifying public goods. As a professor of writing studies at a large university in the Midwest, I am intimately familiar with this bright, largely optimistic view of writing. Proponents of this positive outlook see learning to write effectively as foundational to succeeding in college and critical after college in everything from business to medicine to the creative arts. Those who hold this optimistic view of writing see writers as people who make ethical choices when they write, and those choices are perceived as essential to gaining social autonomy and increased cultural participation. Writing is considered a particularly good medium for persuading others of one's arguments and even sometimes generating complex "understanding across difference." Writing is perceived as a great tool for self-expression, a way to facilitate interpersonal communication, and a medium through which one can develop a public voice. Adherents to this positive view of writing see acts of writing (and revising) as helping writers develop productive habits of mind and fostering critical thinking. Writing is essential to learning, this optimistic outlook suggests, and with practice writers might develop a recognizable and expressive voice. Writers have the freedom to make decisions when they write, and being an *author* can mean gaining *authority*: respect and recognition that is fostered through effective writing and even protected by copyright law. This promising view of writing values carefully crafted written texts for the page, tablet, or screen. But writing can also be personal: maintaining a written journal is seen as a place to "take control" and "engage in independent inquiry," and written correspondence with others fosters richer relationships. Writing, this viewpoint suggests, can do all these things and more as literacy helps to make up the fabric of social life. Not without controversy, literacy scholar Walter Ong has even suggested that "writing restructures consciousness" in several positive ways.[1]

And yet, across a wide array of social domains, acts of writing and written text itself are seen not only as empowering but also as imbued with the power to discipline, shame, and control others. Teachers, judges, parents, university administrators, partiers, sex traffickers, and vigilantes have used writing as punishment. This book studies five different kinds of punishment writing. By examining these practices side by side, I provide a new perspective on the perceived capacity of writing to transform individuals. Writing certainly has the potential to improve, liberate, and empower, but it is also imagined to have an array of more perverse powers in what might be called a punishment-oriented or discipline-based perspective on writing.

As a study about how writing is used to punish, shame, humiliate, and control, this book offers a counterview to beliefs that writing is edifying. However, I do not set out to disprove this more optimistic view of writing so much as complicate it: to illustrate how beliefs in the transformative power of writing fuel both ideals of edification and demoralization. By studying how the major actors in this book (teachers, judges, parents, university administrators, partiers, sex traffickers, and vigilantes) use writing to punish and shame, the practices that define this discipline-based perspective show that some see writing as not all about making choices but about submitting to the mandates and choices of others. Writing is not only seen as good at helping to develop thoughts and ideas but also as a way to become indoctrinated into the beliefs of others. Writing might inspire or cultivate a voice, but it can also dull and drown out individuality, rebelliousness, and agency.

Writing is thought to have such capacities even when it is nonconsensual, and by "writing" I mean being made to write, forcibly associated with a written text, or physically written on. Writing can be a powerful tool for calling someone out and humiliating them before an audience, and it can be used to diminish key aspects of literate agency. In some forms of discipline-based writing, the imposition of a silencing, overriding text can usurp free speech. In other cases, writing defines, controls, and even manages the economic labor of those regulated by it, and it does so while redefining the very identities of victims. Discipline-based writing is thought, by the teachers, judges, and other citizens who deploy it, to enact such lofty things as justice, reform, and rehabilitation. In this discipline-based paradigm, writing is seen as a powerful tool that can undermine, shape, and control those who end up coming into contact with the written word. This book reveals a view of writing that sees it as enacting a potentially volatile transformation on writers.

So how do these two opposing and seemingly competing views on writing—the edifying perspective and the discipline-based one—coexist? They both emerge in part from shared beliefs about the capabilities and affordances of writing. In sharing certain core values and beliefs about what writing is and how it works, I argue that the two perspectives intertwine and perpetually renew one other. They are two sides of the same coin. Even though many of the practices that fall under what I call the discipline-based perspective have been argued against, banned, and in some instances even made illegal in the United States and elsewhere, they have, in most cases, continued to thrive across many cultures for hundreds of years. The fortitude of the various uses of writing as punishment described in this book stems from the fact that such practices are grounded in some of the same beliefs about writing that motivate someone like me to teach college students how to write effective essays and express themselves in writing for an audience. While some of the uses of writing for punishment that I describe in this book are clearly deviant, they share a similar logic about how writing works with more mainstream and accepted uptakes of writing.

The shared beliefs that inform both the edifying and discipline-based views on writing are rooted in the notion that written communication is distinct from other forms of human expression—such as speech, gesture, dance, drawing, painting, or music—and has the intrinsic potential to help develop the minds of writers and those associated with writing. This value placed on written communication in particular informs such things as decisions to use writing to save failing US schools and requirements that nearly all US college students must take a first-year writing course. It is also why the many people described in this book turn to writing, instead of other communicative options, to discipline and punish. For those who use writing as punishment, they often see writing as a way to tap directly into the minds of those being disciplined. I argue that uses of writing as punishment reveal a belief that certain genres, such as the essay and personal letter, have the potential to transform writers on multiple levels, and that belief informs both educational and disciplinary uptakes of writing. If acts of writing were universally seen as nothing more than inconsequential or only busy work, writing would not have such lasting appeal. In short, whether for edification or humiliation, writing is seen as a medium of expression that works on writers as they write on the page.[2]

I highlight these shared beliefs about writing because it would be easy to assume that a book such as this one would condemn the use of writing as punishment. Some of the practices I describe in this book are undoubtedly cruel, while others are merely misguided, but I contend that the edifying perspective and the disciplinary one are merely different uptakes of the same core values and beliefs about writing. Both sides think of writing as a special communicative channel that has the potential to change writers and those affiliated with certain written texts. It is these beliefs that I question in this book. As a study of the use of writing as punishment, what follows is meant to complement the much-lauded edifying perspective on writing with a detailed examination of the somewhat more sinister view that writing is perfectly suited to discipline and punishment. Condemning the use of writing as punishment would be too easy; I prefer to work to understand it.

If you have read J. K. Rowling's series of Harry Potter novels or seen the movies, then you know that Rowling's mystical world has sanctified forms of magic that are taught in school and another body of frowned-upon curses referred to as "the dark arts." Students at Hogwarts School of Witchcraft and Wizardry must take a core course titled "Defense against the Dark Arts," which is intended to protect them from "unforgiveable curses" that are intended to control (*Imperio*), torture (*Crucio*), and kill (*Avada Kedavra*). My exploration of the many ways that writing is used as punishment in the contemporary United States could be compared to an exploration of some of the dark arts of writing. It can be appealing to think of writing as exclusively about developing critical thinking skills and robust forms of interpersonal communication. But across many sectors of society, writing is taken up to accomplish more sinister goals of the rhetorical "dark arts." Punishment writing is used with the hope of vanquishing certain thoughts and inclinations from the minds of others, programming new thoughts, peering deep within the soul of the writer, and even making someone physically embody the written words of another author. In the many uses of writing as punishment, writing is used in efforts to accomplish all of these sinister acts and more. There is even a quasi belief, embedded in some uses of writing as punishment, in writing as having alchemical properties capable of renaming a person, redefining that person's core beliefs, or curbing certain behaviors, as if writing has magical properties.

The case studies in this book fall on either side of a significant dividing line, and recognizing this line should help provide both a sense of how writing is used as punishment and the organizing logic of the book. Three of my chapters (1, 2, and 5) examine writing-based punishments and public shamings meted out by teachers, judges, and parents working within the frameworks of US social institutions of the school, court, and family. These punishments generally use writing to try to teach, reform, redeem, or cure. Said another way, writing is used in these efforts to "improve" the punished. And in these cases, the punishments are represented as in the best interest of the person being punished. In addition, there is a sense in these examples that writing-based punishments are humane, civilized, and sometimes even a privilege. On the other side of this line are two chapters (3 and 4) about people using writing as punishment outside of formal institutions. In these examples—which feature partiers, sex traffickers, and vigilantes—writing is not used so much to cure and redeem as it is to shame, degrade, and control. These are examples of everyday citizens, either acting alone or in crowds, who take up writing to redefine someone, call that person out, or even enact extrajudicial forms of justice.

Another key difference running through this book has to do with different meanings of the capacious term *writing*. Two of the chapters in this book (1 and 5) focus on people being made to actually write for their punishments. In carefully orchestrated writing rituals, sitting down to write is seen as something that has the power to control, shape, and/or create a sort of window into the soul of the writer. And in these examples, writing is generally prescribed or required for its perceived redemptive properties. In chapters 2, 3, and 4, it is not acts of writing that are used so much as written texts themselves, or the written word, in efforts to bring about punishment or public shaming. In these examples, the person being punished does not have to do any actual writing but is instead forced to be affiliated with some kind of written text. In these examples, written texts themselves are thought to exert power: those who are punished are linked to texts in various ways, with the imposed language often nonconsensually speaking for them or through them, often in public spaces.

As you have probably gathered, many of the punishments described in this book use writing to leverage the twin social powers of shame and humiliation. In my examples, both are typically generated by involving audiences, who are meant to read or witness punishment writing. In some cases, such as in drunk shaming, anonymous writers produce shame by acting together on the body of the targeted person. In other examples, a known author imposes shameful writing on the person being punished. Every time shameful scenes appear in this book, they are crafted with slightly different configurations of written text, readers, and authors. In some scenes where writing is used as punishment, shame is minimal, while in others it is quite extreme. In still other examples, writing-based punishments involve eroticized forms of shame and humiliation.[3] I also discuss what has been referred to as the shaming of callout culture, as several of the writing-based punishments in this book share a great deal with social media callouts that silence and publically humiliate online. To contextualize the appealing nature of shame in the US legal context, I turn to current work by legal scholars who have written a good deal about "modern shame punishments."[4] Some judges in the United States have used both acts of writing and written texts to generate shame. It is also worth noting that the shame-based writing punishments I discuss in this book appear on both sides of the law: meted out by criminals and judges alike.

Writing is used as punishment in a wide range of cultural contexts, so this book explores the topic from multiple angles. Most of the chapters rely in some way on news reporting, as writing-based punishments continually "make the news" because they are seen as novel and amusing. Some of these news stories involve criminal uses of writing to shame, control, and punish, so most of the chapters involve discussion of published court documents that describe how writing is used as punishment both in crimes and in response to them. To get a sense of how young people view the kinds of writing on the body that take place in drunk-shaming incidents, I conducted a small qualitative study of undergraduate students on my campus. In addition, scholars working in the fields of psychology, criminology, rhetoric, and sociology have discussed writing-based and similar rituals, so I turn to their research at various points in this book to enhance my readings. Writing-based punishments also surface with some frequency in film and literature, so I incorporate such examples because they provide insights into the potentials and limits of writing-based punishments. Most of the writing rituals I discuss in this book also have historical precedents, so I rely on a variety of historical texts and some primary historical documents to reveal just how long-standing writing-based punishments are. What I hope to have created, through the incorporation of so many disparate views, is a well-researched book that offers an illuminating trek through this widespread fixation with using writing as punishment.

While I have worked to make this research as extensive as possible, it is worth noting that the scope of the book still has a focus. In terms of my argument, I attend to uses of writing in Western, English-speaking cultures. The case studies I explore in most depth come from US schools, courts, and popular culture. With this being said, at times throughout the book, I refer to examples of writing-based punishments and degradation rituals in places as far afield as Germany, India, and China. While this kind of global sampling runs the risk of making ahistorical and decontextualized treatments of writing in those places, I draw upon a small number of global examples to show that my case studies from the United States are not mere anomalies. In terms of my larger discussions of writing as ritual and cultural practice, it is worth noting that the writing practices

I discuss in this book amount to only a very small cross section of the history of writing more broadly. The development of written language has many long and varied histories, from cuneiform tablets to tablet PCs, and I deal with only a few of those forms and contexts of writing in this vast history, highlighting particular ways of thinking about writing as a disciplinary technology.[5]

Chapter 1, "Punishing Children with Writing," opens the book by looking at how some teachers, for more than 150 years, have used different kinds of writing tasks to discipline their students. Students have been made to write potentially redemptive phrases over and over, craft essays and book reports on restorative topics, and even write their own names on the board—all as ways to use writing to reshape and reform them. In each of these schoolhouse punishments, different presumptions about how writing works are leveraged to change the student writer. I start the book with this discussion of writing as punishment in schools because it is in school where many of us first encountered the idea that writing has this potential for social control.

Chapter 2, "Shame Parades," deals with the practice of punishing people by making them hold or wear signs in public. This form of punishment has existed for hundreds of years across many different cultures, and in the chapter, I focus on contemporary instances of judges and parents who have made adults and children stand in public bearing condemnatory signs. Shame parades, as these scenes are sometimes called, involve the use of writing to shame, punish, and humiliate both by silencing the person with the sign and making him or her "speak publically," in a sense, involuntarily.

Chapter 3, "Writing on the Wasted," explores another form of involuntary speech that takes place on the actual body of the person targeted. In this chapter, the people being punished and shamed have been written on while unconscious, so they literally embody various messages on their skin. The social practice known as drunk shaming involves writing that is always physically intimate and frequently profane. Elaborate rules govern how this social ritual takes place, and in this chapter, I draw upon the small study I conducted on my college campus.

Chapter 4, "Forced Tattooing," looks at the even more intense and disturbing practice in which victims are forcibly tattooed with words, phrases, and other symbols. The chapter shows how, in the domain of sex trafficking, the tattoos simultaneously change a victim's identity, demean her, and also maintain a system of managed economic control. To make sense of this practice, I discuss some of the extended histories of forced tattooing and also explain contemporary cases of forcibly applied tattoos that are used for extrajudicial justice.

Chapter 5, "Writing, Self-Reflection, and Justice," returns to the scene of the courtroom to describe cases in which judges have required defendants to write letters of apology, essays, and book reports. These punishments have some similarity to the ones described in chapter 1 about schoolhouse punishments, but the difference here is that when judges demand punishment writing, such legal sentences actually have aspects of privilege built into them. I also discuss the legal philosophy of restorative justice that has come to inform the use of apology letter writing in some court cases.

In my conclusion to the book, I focus on a dilemma that pervades this book: How can those of us who value writing and use it "for good" do so for some of the same reasons that motivate those who use writing for punishment? I provide what I think are some ways of reconciling this dilemma based on what I see as the main things we can learn from a study of writing as punishment.

The many ways that writing has been used as punishment have never been hidden, as these writing rituals almost always rely on an audience: writing has been used as punishment in public places such as schools, city streets, parties, and courts of law. But what has remained hidden is how these punishments and shamings have close connections to more seemingly edifying, educational, and mainstream uses of writing. This book aims to explore the underside of "good writing," unveiling beliefs that writing is simultaneously dangerous and redemptive. By understanding the logic behind the use of writing as punishment, we get closer to understanding some of the deepest, most entrenched beliefs about why writing matters.

ONE

PUNISHING CHILDREN WITH WRITING

Writing lines is the penance Harrovians [students at an all-boys school in London]
do for all their sins, in and out of school. If a boy is late for school, he writes lines; if
he misses "bill," he writes lines. If the lines are not finished at the stated time, their
number is doubled. There was one clever boy who escaped writing half the ordered
quantity; and the master tells the story of how he did it to this day.
                    —Elizabeth Robins Pennell, 1887, "Harrow-on-the-Hill"

It is a curious fact that writing has long been used to punish schoolchildren. I say that it is curious because teaching students to write effectively
has simultaneously been held up as an important educational goal. Writing-
based punishments do not aim to make better writers, and yet, they are
one way some teachers use writing in schools. Learning to write effectively
is often described to students as "necessary later in life" for communi-
cating and performing any number of workplace tasks, and yet, writing-
based punishments model very different purposes for writing: according
to these punishments, writing is a process of submitting to authority and
something that promises to change you against your will. In a world where
written works by authors such as William Shakespeare and Jane Austen are
celebrated and the "language arts" of reading and writing are seen as potentially sophisticated, challenging, and redemptive, schoolhouse discipline
via writing as punishment seems to give writing a more sinister quality.

In this chapter, I explore how the writing-based punishments used to
control and discipline students reveal particular beliefs about the capabilities of writing as a means of discipline and control. These classroom punishments also reveal that punishment writing can become involved in the
power dynamics of the classroom, mediating between teachers who believe
in the potential of nonconsensual writing and students who are forced to
engage in carefully orchestrated acts of solitary writing.

I begin this book with this chapter on the use of writing as punishment in schools because the classroom is a sort of birthplace for how and why writing is thought to work so successfully as a tool for punishment, shame, ridicule, and humiliation in and across the many other contexts and situations I describe in this book. The long tradition of punishing children with writing, and calling them out on the chalkboard, serves as a constantly renewed source for the much wider cultural belief that writing has the coercive ability to punish. Understanding the mechanisms behind the use of writing as punishment in schools provides a foundation for understanding similar uses of writing that take place far from the classroom. For most of us, we were schoolchildren ourselves when we first encountered the idea that writing can be used not only for learning but also for discipline and punishment. Even if you were not made to write something like "I will not chew gum in class" fifty, one hundred, or one thousand times yourself, you may have witnessed one of your classmates writing lines of some kind or being punished by having to craft a mandated letter of apology or punitive essay. Seeing and experiencing these uses of writing teaches lessons, I argue, about the imagined powers of writing.

As the chapter develops, I avoid the unanswerable question of the effectiveness of the use of writing as punishment and instead explore such uses of writing as social practices that reveal a good deal about cultural and rhetorical beliefs. Punishing children by having them write actually makes visible a widely held belief that writing can exercise a kind of power over writers that is not found in spoken discourse. The uses of writing as punishment in schools suggest that particular acts of writing, if orchestrated in just the right ways, have the power to transform writers. So, I set out in this chapter to explain why this message has been propagated for so long in our schools through the persistent use of writing as punishment. Why would writing be figured as so transformative, disciplinary, and powerful—particularly when using it for punishment tends to strike many as not really that effective? Many forms of punishment writing have been satirized and critiqued as emblematic of sham forms of schoolhouse justice and control. And yet, the practice continues.

I say that writing is special in having a mystique of disciplinary power because, when compared against the many other educational activities students engage in on a daily basis, writing has been most elaborately adapted and repurposed for use as punishment. As the epigraph to this chapter indicates, over a hundred years ago in the 1800s, writing resided beside the paddle and the dunce cap in the arsenal of punishment tools used by many teachers. Even as paddles and dunce caps have fallen from favor, punishment writing has remained a viable disciplinary technique. In one study from the 1980s, over half of teachers polled indicated a familiarity with the use of writing as punishment in schools.[1] Writing as a form of punishment has survived as long as it has because, in part, it has an aura of civility and because it is still seen as at least marginally effective. In the course of any given day, across the many academic subjects students pursue, they are asked to do such things as complete math problems, create graphs, conduct science experiments, draw maps, give speeches, conduct research, make art, play, exercise, and write. And while I have come across some examples of students being required to complete math problems as punishment or do physical exercise as punishment, no other single academic activity has been repurposed as punishment to the degree that writing has. Think about it: having a student create a piece of art or make a graph as a form of punishment seems absurd in comparison to having that same student write an essay or compose a letter of apology about what he or she did wrong. It is easy to take for granted that writing, of all things, is viable as a form of punishment, and my purpose here is to explore why.

I am not the first person to point out that getting students to appreciate writing does not exactly jibe with punishing them with it. I spend some time in this chapter describing how, starting in the mid-nineteenth century, arguments began to be made against the use of punishment writing in schools. Critiques of teachers who use writing as punishment in their classrooms have gone on for over a hundred years, with various self-appointed "protectors of writing" having tried hard to do away with this particular use of writing. As I describe, some scholars of rhetoric and writing have framed writing instruction in particular as having a moral component and see writing's very nature as being about ethical deliberation.[2] Writing-based punishments (especially ones based on composing tedious, repetitive, involuntarily selected utterances) challenge these moral and ethical perspectives on writing. But despite attacks on the use of writing as punishment, these punishment methods continue to appeal to some teachers.

In schools and across our cultures, there are a wide range of entrenched cultural beliefs about writing. There is the belief that literacy is an essential component of good citizenship, the belief that learning to write well can help lead to success later in life, and the belief that becoming literate is essential to higher-level reasoning.[3] Another set of less thoroughly examined beliefs about writing are encrypted in and reproduced through the use of writing as punishment, and these are the beliefs that writing is a viable tool for disciplining, controlling, brainwashing, shaming, demeaning, subjugating, and humiliating others. Forcing someone to write particular things in particular ways establishes power and control in a seemingly simple use of compulsory literacy. In schools, the sordid history of using writing as punishment has long marked writing as having the potential to undermine the power and authority of writers, and this has positioned writing as having a special kind of power and mystique. And as I describe, some of the basis for using writing as punishment involves the idea that the act of writing something down on paper is believed to act back on writers as if by magic not just rhetoric.

CEREMONIES OF PUNISHMENT WRITING IN SCHOOLS

Of the many methods described in this book for punishing, shaming, humiliating, and controlling with writing, only a few of those methods are used on children. Very particular writing rituals have been adapted and fine-tuned for the use on children in schools. I use the word *ritual* here to make the point that the ways writing has been used as a punishment are, like other rituals, imbued with cultural meaning. There are many descriptions of what cultural rituals are and how they function, but my thinking about punishment writing as having ritualistic aspects is best captured in Jeffrey Alexander's explanation of ritual. He writes: "Rituals are episodes of repeated and simplified cultural communication in which the direct partners to a social interaction, and those observing it, share a mutual belief in the . . . communication's symbolic contents and accept the authenticity of one another's intentions. It is because of this shared understanding of intention and content, and in the intrinsic validity of the interaction, that rituals have their effect and affect."[4] To translate this definition of ritual over to uses of writing as punishment, the "simplified cultural communication" is the scene of a student being punished by having to write in some way; and the "partners to a social interaction" and "those observing it" are the teacher, punished student, and other witnesses (typically students). The act of punishing a student with writing is not simply an exercise in writing something down, "the communication" has "symbolic contents" that resonate because of a "shared understanding" of what punishment writing means. As Alexander describes, "rituals have their effect and affect," and both resonate through the use of writing as punishment, informing shared views on what writing is and how it works.

In the ritualistic use of writing as punishment, how writing is coupled with discipline is not random. Very particular orchestrations of writing tap into what are seen as the less resistible, more controlling powers and capabilities that writing is imagined—through the function of ritual—to have. These writing rituals have been developed and maintained over time for the use of writing as punishment, and the use of established, long-lasting rituals has helped maintain the beliefs that writing in certain ways can actually discipline, redeem, and alter the writer. This is at least what the use of writing as punishment, as a ritual, expresses to those who experience and witness it. Encrypted in the particularities of these schoolhouse traditions are core beliefs about writing as a potentially dark, magical rhetorical art capable of punishing, controlling, and transforming writers.

Elizabeth Robins Pennell did not see students writing poems or short stories for their punishments in the 1880s, and they certainly were not engaging in free-writes about their innermost feelings. They were not drawing, dancing, or reciting lines. Instead, students writing lines caught her attention, and this type of writing is the most iconic and recognizable form of ritualized punishment writing. I could fill this entire book with anecdotes about students having to write lines in schools over the past 150 years. In the interest of space, I will give just a few examples of the use and adaptation over time of this particular form of punishment writing.

In 1898 in the British periodical *Public School Magazine*, an anonymous student describes the punishment this way: "Some masters have a wonderful aptitude for inventing long lines with curious words, while others content themselves with picking out five or six of the longest words in the language and give you such a line as 'Incorrigible irregularity necessitates drastic treatment,' and then, with that cool impudence which only masters possess, they insist on your doing 600 of them because there are only five words in the line, and that is what they call being lenient." In a remembrance of going to a private Catholic school in California in the 1950s, a former student describes how "if we did something horrid, like writing a name on the wall in the bathroom, we had to 'write lines' during lunch, which meant we ate in the classroom, could not go outside to play and had to write 100, 500, or 1,000 times." And in a 1994 court case involving a legal appeal by a dismissed teacher, one witness's testimony claimed that, after the teacher accused an entire seventh-grade class of "talking in the lunch line," the teacher made all of the students write lines. In an even more recent account from the UK in 2014, a twelve-year-old schoolgirl reports being "forced to write 'decent people take pride in their appearance' 40 times after turning up to school in the wrong shoes." Writing lines has even been updated for technology-savvy millennials: in a widely shared news story from 2016, students in a school in Chengdu, China, were reportedly made to write out one thousand emojis for arriving late to class. So writing lines has existed across time and place with little variation, and while this particular punishment technique does not seem to be as common now in schools as it was in the nineteenth century, it remains a form of punishment used by some teachers.[5]

Having to write lines—also referred to as "rote writing" or having to complete "a writing imposition"—is also the most frequently satirized form of schoolhouse punishment writing. Each episode of *The Simpsons* television show begins with Bart Simpson writing lines on a chalkboard at the front of his classroom, as rote punishment writing has become a symbol of futile, old-fashioned, one-size-fits-all schoolhouse discipline. Writing in the 1980s about this form of punishment, Linda Brodkey suggests that "the task itself seems designed to make nonsense out of writing, for the punishment usually consists in writing the same sentence a set number of times. Children, of course, are inclined to enact the punishment in ways that call attention to its absurdity. It is not unusual, for instance, for a child to complete the task vertically rather than horizontally. Thus, the punishment sentence, 'I will not talk in class,' is reproduced in columns: a column for 'I,' a column for 'will,' and so on."[6] Even while writing lines is easily mocked in popular culture and thwarted by students who are punished this way, decoding how this practice is thought to work reveals several key beliefs about writing as a tool for social control.

When made to write lines, the student is typically forced to compose (usually with a pen or pencil; seldom via a typewriter or word processor) simple, declarative sentences that relate to the violation. So talking out in class is met with sentences about respecting others, and tardiness is met with sentences about punctuality. This relationship between what is written and the punishment stems from a core belief that as we write on the page, what we write is written back on us. This is the almost magical power I have been referring to: the belief that there is an inherent bidirectionality to writing.

Now, if writing has a bidirectional power, it is not thought to be perfect. This is why students who are punished in this way do not have to craft long sentences with complex structures such as dependent clauses and hedging (e.g., "I will not chew gum in class, unless it is a day when we have a test and . . ."). In rote writing, simple sentences are imagined to be more likely to transfer back onto the writer, and they are repeated over and over again because the marks that writing leaves need time, apparently, to "sink in." No one believes that writing "I will respect my teacher" just once will do the job, but can such a message be resistible after five hundred or one thousand times? With enough repetition, what is written down just might sink in.

This belief in writing as working almost magically in two directions at once—upon the page and back on the writer—is satirized and explored in two pieces of fiction published almost a century apart. These fictional accounts vividly show a power dynamic in which the punisher believes in the bidirectional capabilities of writing and the punished resist this pseudomagical power. In a 1919 short story by Czech writer Franz Kafka, titled "In the Penal Colony," an explorer visits a penal colony to find that convicted criminals are routinely strapped to a large "apparatus" that violently cuts written punishment sentences into their bodies. The apparatus uses a writing implement that is as sharp as a knife, and the condemned eventually bleed to death. In Kafka's story, "the Officer," a champion of this gruesome process of writing on the bodies of the condemned, insists that being sentenced in this way brings about a kind of cathartic transformation before death. In a similarly bloody scene from J. K. Rowling's *Harry Potter and the Order of the Phoenix* (2003), the young wizard Harry Potter is unjustly accused of lying and made to write lines with an enchanted quill. As Harry Potter writes out his punishment lines, the magical quill cuts into his hand and extracts his blood, using it as ink. Magically, the pen also carves the words back on Harry Potter as he writes "I must not tell lies."

These two fictional accounts take a figurative belief—that writing has the power to work back on the writer—and enact it literally on the bodies of the punished. In both fictional accounts, it is important to note that this belief about writing is also exposed as absurd and ineffective; the contents of the written messages never really sink into the minds of the punished. So too are real world uses of writing lines often seen as an absurd form of punishment with no real potential for inscribing new beliefs upon writers. Nonetheless, rote writing maintains some power over the writers who must submit to the lines. Even as this form of punishment writing fails to perfectly instill new beliefs in punished writers, it continues to get used—and this use perpetuates the belief that writing has very real and tangible bidirectional powers.

It is not just when students are made to write lines that writing is thought to work back on the minds of writers but also when they are punished with copy writing. In cases when copy writing is used for punishment, a student might be made to copy pages of a textbook, say, or (as I witnessed while working as a student teacher in Seattle in the 1990s) the classroom attendance policy after arriving late to class. In another example, this one from a 2013 lawsuit involving a private school in Toronto, students were "made to copy out the school's code of conduct by hand for two hours as punishment."[7] Copy writing relies on the same logic that repetitive writing will "sink in," as is the case with writing lines, only the difference is that there is never any assumption that the student must do any original composing for him or her to undergo transformation via the punishment. Merely copying down something already written is framed, in copy writing as punishment, as having the power to imprint previously formed ideas on the consciousness of the copyist-student-writer who is being punished. In the imagined workings of this power dynamic, the student is made to submit to codified knowledge by the teacher.

Another belief running through all of these punishments is so fundamental to them that it ends up informing every other form of punishment writing discussed in the book. This belief is closely related to the assumed bidirectional powers of writing, and it is so ubiquitous and taken for granted that it is easily overlooked. It is simply the notion that written language is fundamentally unlike other forms and channels of human expression, giving it a special power to act upon and transform the writer. Writing something down, in this sense, is imagined as fundamentally different from speaking even the exact same words. The long-standing use of writing for punishment—not speaking or visual forms of expression or even gestural communication—reveals this belief that writing certain things in certain ways can be transformative. By relation, speaking or signing or expressing language in some other way is construed as less powerful and less substantial.

If it was believed that linguistically expressing an idea in any way had transformative potential, then one would only have to utter or even think a phrase once—"I will not chew gum" or "I will respect my classmates"—for the imagined transformation to take place. But it seems absurd to imagine that orally stating a viewpoint once would cause anyone to adopt some new idea or belief, and yet it seems somehow less absurd to think that writing that viewpoint down might do exactly that. Classroom uses of writing as punishment stem from and reveal this belief that written modes of expression transform in ways others do not. In my research for this book, I did not encounter a single example of a student being made to repeat a phrase aloud for punishment—uttering something like "I will not chew gum" or "I will respect the teacher"—whereas, I have found countless examples of students being made to write down such simple sentences. Using writing for these punishments, instead of other forms of human expression, couples writing with discipline and continues to imbue writing with an aura of transformative power.

This notion that writing has very particular powers is not entirely unfounded; in fact, a body of research has shown that writing can help people remember things. In a variety of different research studies, writing things down has been shown to help writers recall concepts and prior events. In one such study, those who wrote down unfamiliar words—as opposed to just hearing them—were more likely to recall the terms later. In another study, undergraduates who wrote about topics that were personally interesting to them remembered more than a control group. But this research also shows that not all forms of writing help us remember in the same ways. In response to the recent rise of laptop computers for notetaking in college classrooms, one study showed that writing with a pen or pencil actually aided memory more than keyboarding/typing, in part because those who typed their notes typed up everything they heard, as opposed to translating their notes into shorthand. So it has been shown that writing can generally help writers remember things, but it is a big leap between using writing to remember something and using writing to instill new beliefs or ideas in an unwilling writer.[8]

Writing-based punishments aim to reprogram deviant students, making them "good" and rule abiding. In the case of a student who arrives late to class, say, the student was not necessarily tardy because he or she forgot there was a rule about tardiness. For this reason, copying the definition of the word *punctual* from the dictionary is not simply intended to help the student remember what that word means. The writing punishment is a way to get the student to submit, via writing, to the teacher.

Rituals of punishment writing in schools do not all involve endless repetition, as ritualized forms of writing punishment also entail having students write such things as reflective and argumentative essays, reports, and letters of apology.[9] All of these forms of mandated writing—*not* poems or short stories or lists but genres such as essays, reports, and letters of apology—engage students in the creation of very particular kinds of texts for the purposes of their discipline and punishment. Similar beliefs inform this more expository branch of punishment writing: namely the notion that the content of what a student writes has the potential to "sink in" when the ideas are written down—even in an involuntary writing task. Writing is imagined as having the ability to overpower the will of the writer, for instance, and to create new and genuine thoughts and dispositions. In these forms of mandated writing, the repetition and simplicity found in rote writing and copy writing are done away with. Instead of penning simple phrases over and over, complex writing tasks are forced upon the writer. Some of the logic behind this kind of punishment seems to be that if writing an essay or report can demonstrate learning in an academic context, then why not adopt that form of writing to make the student "learn a lesson" as punishment. This is why, in *Arkansas Department of Human Services v. Caldwell* (and legal cases like it), testimony reveals how three fifth-grade school girls who were caught smoking were made to "write a report on smoking."[10] In a sense, this kind of punishment endorses a larger belief in the value of expository writing, but it remains imagined that the punished writer cannot somehow resist the power of the writing activity.

In developing a full catalog of different types of schoolhouse punishment writing, it is worth mentioning the age-old practice of writing student names on the board—as this kind of writing-based punishment has a logic all its own. It seems like a simple act: a student speaks out of turn in class or breaks some other rule, and the student's name is written on the board. In some accounts of this punishment, the teacher writes the name; in others, the student is made to walk to the front of the room and write his or her own name on the board. Either way, the goal is to call attention to the student and exercise some level of control over the student via the written name.

In the contemporary world of networked social media, "chalkboards" have become sites such as Facebook and Twitter, and drawing attention to someone by name is known as a callout. Such callouts on social media often condemn stereotypical, racist, sexist, or otherwise offensive speech. Writing for the *Stranger*, language and social critic Katie Herzog lashes out against the silencing nature of callout culture, arguing that it "prevents people from actually speaking their minds, because they are too scared of being unfriended, unfollowed, blocked, shunned, or dismissed as simply trash." In a sense, writing a student's name on a chalkboard is intended to exercise control over a student in a related way, but what happens in the classroom works through a simpler mechanism than a social media callout. On social media, a callout will typically engage with the original behavior or speech; in the classroom, all that is needed is a name on the chalkboard for the student to become visibly called out before the whole class.[11]

In a 2006 Ohio lawsuit claiming that a teacher had abused a student, the plaintiff testified that the teacher's extreme punishments began with writing the student's name on the board: "So she got up and told me to write my name on the board, and I did, and she got mad at me." In another case where a teacher was ultimately dismissed, the teacher started by calling the student out via the board: "Ms. Fuller began to write J-C's name on the board whenever he did something wrong." I mention these cases not to suggest that writing a student's name on the board is always associated with more serious forms of teacher abuse; instead, these extreme cases show how a name on the board is a familiar part of a larger, if in these instances misguided, system of classroom discipline.[12]

Note that this kind of classroom discipline does not involve the student engaging in much if any writing, as the other forms of writing-based punishment do, but a name on the board tries to accomplish more than merely keeping track of a student's infractions. Writing student names on the board, in the most basic sense, associates the simple act of writing something down with establishing disciplinary power. At the risk of making too much of the common practice of writing a student's name on the board, I see this as one more way that rituals of writing—here it is just a written name; in the other cases I have discussed, much more elaborate and expressive acts of writing are used—inextricably bind writing with power, control, and in this case public humiliation. The name is written on the board at the front of the classroom to draw negative attention to the student, and this same theme reappears in much more serious acts of writing on the body discussed later. Through having one's name written on the board, the student is immediately associated with shame and wrongdoing via writing. The mere act of writing J-C's name on the board is an attempt to discipline him, and the instrument of control is writing. While nothing of any real substance is written, no exposition is thought to sink in, and there is no repetition, writing is used to shine a literate light on and bring negative attention to the student, publically shaming him or her before the class.

So, those are several ways that writing is and has been used to punish and control children. It has been used in efforts to imprint students with teacher-approved messages, to get students to think in new ways, to make them submit to a teacher's authority, to publically humiliate them, and to call them out in front of their peers. All the while—since at least the 1860s—self-proclaimed defenders of writing have worked to abolish the use of writing as punishment in the classroom. In what follows, I describe the nature of the battle, waged by educators against educators over the use of writing as punishment. The fight reveals that many of the beliefs informing the use of writing as punishment are in fact *shared* by those who would like to abolish it.

THE OPPOSITION: EFFORTS TO MAKE PUNISHMENT WRITING EXTINCT

Both those in favor of writing as punishment and those who are opposed to it largely seem to agree that having students write can transform them, and that writing is a powerful tool, meaning that both sides in this debate share some of the same values and beliefs (real or imagined) about writing. While the opposition characterizes using writing as punishment as nefarious and degrading to students, I have come to see the various uses of punishment writing as persisting for as long as they have because the values and beliefs that undergird such punishments remain so widespread and unquestioned. By looking at this history of critique, we also find that the opposition has never merely dismissed or viewed as inconsequential the use of writing as punishment. Instead, this form of punishment has garnered the attention of opposing critics who think punishment writing does real damage to students and their beliefs in literacy.

The first public critique of the use of writing as punishment that I have found was published in 1868. In a report released in Britain by the Schools Inquiry Commission, the report's authors conclude that "nothing ruins the hand [i.e., handwriting] so swiftly and surely as the practice of writing impositions." (As I mentioned earlier, "writing impositions" is another term for writing lines.) Writing instruction in the nineteenth century often overlapped with handwriting instruction, which involved the copious copying of original texts (in English, Latin, and Greek). In fact, student notebooks were often referred to as copy books during this period. The authors of the report portray writing as punishment as an adulteration of more noble and educative forms of copying and writing.[13]

Ten years later, in the October 1879 issue of the US publication *Popular Science Monthly* (the precursor to *Popular Science*), author George J. Romanes sets aside the previous argument about handwriting to suggest that using writing as punishment damages a student's mental health: "For the whole punishment of writing out an imposition consists in the tediousness of the process; and tediousness, by the painful class of emotions which it arouses, is the most wearisome or exhausting of influences that consume the nervous energies. It may therefore be said that in whatever degree the writing of an imposition is a punishment, in that degree are the nervous energies dissipated in a wholly useless manner." Romanes's point is that while this kind of punishment might seem harmless, it is far from being in the best interest of children. This implies the notion that, if writing impositions can damage the nerves, then writing in the proper ways can maintain or even strengthen them. In line with this, Frederick Churchill argues in an article titled "High-Pressure Education," published six years later in 1885, that "writing lines is very bad for the healthy and moral training of boys at school. . . . Writing lines unhinges a boy for his proper work." Churchill makes the case that this kind of punishment degrades health and morals. Note that these authors do not dismiss punishment writing as silly or insignificant but see it as having real danger and importance. These critics agree that writing is of great consequence, whether the teacher's intention be to punish or edify.[14]

Critiques of punishment writing continued on through the late nineteenth century, as this kind of punishment remained popular. In an 1893 address to the Teacher's Guild of Great Britain and Ireland, titled "Work and Overwork in Relation to Schools," Clement Dukes (another advocate for student health) made this plea against the use of writing as punishment: "School impositions are of various kinds: but the one that concerns us most to-day and the one chiefly in vogue is that senseless plan unworthy of teachers of writing lines. It does not improve the mind or elevate the character. It certainly spoils the handwriting and is physically harmful to the body in that it deprives the culprit of requisite fresh air and mental rest. I would earnestly appeal to this influential body of teachers to devise some punishment more worthy of an intelligent and noble profession and more in harmony with common sense." Dukes combines the "it destroys handwriting" argument with the "it is bad for their health" critique, clearly wanting to preserve writing tasks as opportunities to "improve the mind" and "elevate the character." In making his impassioned argument against the use of writing as punishment, Dukes characterizes writing-based punishment as demeaning to the entire teaching profession. He appeals to professionalism, claiming that truly professional teachers would not debase writing with such methods.[15]

Flash forward one hundred years to 1985, and the use of writing as punishment is under fire again. Michael Hogan published a study in that year gathering teachers' perceptions of the prevalence of writing for punishment in US schools. Of the teachers surveyed, Hogan found that "over half of the respondents, 54%, indicated awareness of some use of writing to discipline students." Hogan's study showed that "teachers aware of punitive uses of writing indicated that it occurred very frequently (3.4%), frequently (23.7%), sometimes (40.7%), infrequently (20.3%), or rarely (11.9%)." So while writing-based punishments were not thought to be used as often as some describe in the nineteenth century, this form of discipline was far from being nonexistent.[16]

Coinciding with Hogan's report, some 120 years after the Schools Inquiry Commission report of 1868, members of the National Council of Teachers of English (NCTE) crafted a resolution to voice their collective opposition to

the use of writing as punishment in schools. The participating members of
the NCTE framed the problem somewhat differently from how their prede-
cessors had, ignoring the possible degradation of student handwriting and
health and instead focusing on what they perceived as the damage punishment writing was doing to how students view writing. In their "Resolution
on Condemning the Use of Writing as Punishment," the members of the
NCTE stated that using writing as a form of punishment "distorts the principles and defeats the purposes of instruction in this important life skill."
The resolution goes on to insist that using writing for punishment "causes
students to dislike an activity necessary to their intellectual development
and career success." Using writing as punishment, according to this resolution, turns students off to writing and has grave consequences in reducing
a student's future chance of success. In a sense, it is said to be unethical.[17]

As Craig Gibson has shown in his research on ancient Greek and Roman
progymnasmata, which were elaborate speech-writing exercises, there has
long been a moral component to education on the whole and rhetorical
education in particular. Students were not just learning to compose effective speeches in the early progymnasmata exercises; they were learning
to develop the kind of moral character that came from working through
complex dilemmas about such things as good and evil, right and wrong.
John Duffy expresses a similar perspective, characterizing writing and
writing instruction as inextricable from ethical deliberation: "To write is to
make choices, and to teach writing is to teach rationales for making such
choices." For Duffy, you do not have to teach expressly about ethics to teach
ethical decision making—as long as you are teaching writing. Writing-
based punishments, however, leave little room for the kinds of choices
Duffy describes. In most writing-based punishment scenarios, to write is
not to make choices. To write is to comply. For Duffy, "[as] teachers of writing we are always already engaged in the teaching of rhetorical ethics and,
. . . the teaching of writing necessarily and inevitably moves us into ethical
reflections and decision-making." It is no wonder, then, that writing-based
punishments have been critiqued as dulling, unsophisticated, and antithet-
ical to a robust moral and ethical education. Said another way, the many
uses of writing as punishment in schools threaten the view that writing is
intrinsically moral and ethical within the context of schools. In the case of
writing as punishment, writing becomes an act of submission.[18]

In part because of the long history of using writing as punishment and
in part because of the growing history of critique of this kind of discipline,
the use of writing as punishment has become associated with traditional,

back-to-basics approaches to schoolhouse discipline—oddly giving it some renewed support. This revival of punishment writing as an important instrument of (nostalgic) schoolhouse discipline became apparent in 2014, when Great Britain's Department for Education, then headed by conservative politician and education secretary Michael Gove, published a bulletin titled "Behaviour and Discipline in Schools: Advice for Headteachers and School Staff." The document intended to reestablish the powers that headmasters, teachers, and other school staff have when it comes to disciplining students in British schools. The fifteen-page document attempted to grant teachers greater authority and power over students by firmly stating that "poor behaviour" should be addressed with traditional punishments. "When poor behaviour is identified," the bulletin reads, "sanctions should be implemented consistently and fairly in line with the behaviour policy." The list of approved punishments includes such things as detention, lost privileges, and the use of writing as punishment. "Written tasks as punishments" should be utilized, the bulletin suggests, giving examples "such as writing lines or an essay."[19]

In response to the publication of these new policies, several newspapers in the UK ran stories about the guidelines, with the *Daily Mail* interpreting the bulletin as an attempt to push Britain back to a previous era of education: "School pupils face a return to the days of writing out a hundred times 'I will not talk in class' under plans by Education Secretary Michael Gove to return to old-fashioned discipline in the classroom."[20] And this back-to-basics approach was criticized by liberal politicians who took the opportunity to condemn the approach as overly conservative. Gove, a well-known conservative, was under fire, and the use of writing as punishment became a flashpoint issue once again.

In suggesting that the caliber of education offered by British schools could be improved by returning to traditional methods of classroom discipline and by arguing that using writing as punishment is essential to that change, the bulletin imbues mandated writing—forced lines and compulsory essays—with special powers that are constructed as having the ability to change and control students, foster discipline, and manage an unruly student population. Gove's bulletin is nostalgic for a time when it is imagined that strict and powerful teachers ruled their classrooms and student resistance was futile. The use of writing as punishment is seen as an important part of that nostalgic educational dream. Punishment writing is not just another approach to discipline, equivalent to any other; it is symbolic of an imagined era when teachers were thought to control and change the minds and actions of their of students via nothing more than writing exercises. In this nostalgic view of orderly schoolrooms, writing is seen as a powerful disciplinary tool used to control and instruct, manage and inculcate, forcing students to adopt values via the ordered movements of their very own pens and pencils. As Gove's bulletin suggests, liberal-minded educators had abandoned the harmless yet effective instrument of punishment writing.

CAN WRITING BE SAVED?

Punishing students by having them write is certainly not the most wicked or sadistic form of classroom discipline, and it is not even the worst way that writing is used to punish, shame, and humiliate others. In fact, many view the use of writing as punishment in schools as harmless or just plain silly. Where I now live and work, in Illinois, I have heard stories from local middle-school students of kids getting in trouble in school and having to "write a reflection." "It's stupid," one student told me. "You just write it up and it doesn't mean anything." Such has long been one perspective on the use of writing as punishment: that it is no more than a silly and insignificant way to have students kill time and do something they do not want to do—which is write. "You wasted my time, so I'm wasting yours" is a familiar rationale of overworked and exhausted teachers in search of a way to justify classroom discipline.

But I want to insist that the use of writing as punishment in schools is not merely trivial but instead significant in that it stems from and works to produce certain values and beliefs about writing. Overt values about learning to write well figure writing as "an important life skill" that is essential if students are to "get ahead" and succeed in society. The ritualized uses of writing as punishment construe the "life skill" of writing as one that can also involve disempowering others. "Getting ahead" with writing might even involve brainwashing. The use of writing as punishment construes writing as having powers to control, discipline, shame, call out, and punish—and because of the different uses of writing as punishment, these beliefs are rolled into more popular narratives about writing. And for those punished with writing, writing becomes not only an exercise in critical thinking but an occasion for simply doing what one is told. It is ironic that writing is construed as pointlessly rudimentary in some writing-based punishments and also as extraordinarily powerful, almost alchemical stuff. Those who have long opposed the use of writing as punishment also see writing as powerful and important. One group sees writing as transformative for writers, so they want to use it for discipline; the other sees writing as transformative, so they want to keep writing from being corrupted by its use as punishment. And so it is that the use of writing as punishment has remained so popular because of an intrinsic, almost magical belief that writing has special powers to change writers. Recall what John Duffy said: "The teaching of writing necessarily and inevitably moves us into ethical reflections and decision-making." If writing "I will not chew gum in class" over and over again involves ethical decision making, perhaps it is the decision to submit to the will of the teacher's demands.

The simple truth is that it is too late to save writing from those who want to use it to punish children. As this book goes on to show, teachers are not alone: judges, partiers, pimps, and vigilantes have turned to writing as a way to punish, subdue, control, shame, and own. Perhaps they all learned to see writing as a good tool for punishment back in school, or perhaps school teachers have long expressed broader cultural beliefs about writing through their uses of writing as punishment. Either way, there are many other writing rituals that construe writing as imbued with special powers. We just learn about it in school.

TWO

SHAME PARADES

[Cesar] Chavez attended 27 different schools before he reached the eighth grade because his family worked the fields and moved often to find work. As a result, he never could successfully acquire the English language and he was isolated and tormented in school by having to wear a sign around his neck that read, "I am a clown. I speak Spanish."

      —Lina Bell Soares and Karen Wood, "A Critical Literacy Perspective"

In 2012, on the social image sharing site Tumblr, users began sharing images of dogs and handwritten signs. The signs were either next to the dogs or the dogs were wearing them slung around their necks on string (fig. 2.1). What each sign said was different, but the general theme was the same: the signs all referred to something naughty the dogs had done. "I hid meat in the couch," "I climbed into the UPS truck and peed on the packages," "I ate an entire bag of Skittles." That kind of thing.

These images of naughty dogs and their signs quickly became an Internet meme, with new versions appearing daily and circulating widely online. Images of the dogs started to be called "dog shaming," and cat-shaming images quickly followed. In little time, dedicated dog-shaming websites had sprung up, and by 2013, one could buy a dog-shaming book or calendar on Amazon.com. Dog shaming had gone viral.

These dog-shaming images are simultaneously cute, funny, and a little bit sad. The dogs pose calmly for their photos, and it is easy to imagine that some of the dogs look shamefaced. Other dogs appear oblivious to their crimes even when they are photographed surrounded by evidence of their wrongdoing: things such as tattered couch cushions and shredded clothing litter the photos. I say the images are a little bit sad because the signs appear to speak for the dogs, admitting their guilt, but the dogs do not know what they are being made to say.

Figure 2.1. An example of a typical dog-shaming image from www.dog-shame.com.

When the dog-shaming meme blew up on the Internet in 2012 and 2013, the images seemed new and clever—like so many things online. But dog-shaming images actually borrow from and take part in a long-standing tradition of using written signs to humiliate and shame people in public. In dog shaming, writing ventriloquizes a confessional, putting words in the dog's mouth. Sign shaming works the same when people are involved: it uses writing to reduce the person being shamed, if only for a short while, exclusively to what is written on the sign. In this form of punishment, writing takes rhetorical agency away from the person being punished, and whoever reads the sign becomes complicit in the act of punishment.

Cesar Chavez, as the epigraph to this chapter indicates, was humiliated with a sign strung around his neck by a school teacher in the late 1930s or early 1940s. Outside of the US context, "shame parades" became a tradition in China until, in 2010, the Ministry of Public Security put an end to the practice.[1] In Chinese shame parades, groups of accused or convicted criminals (often all of one type: so a group of prostitutes or a group of thieves) were paraded through city streets wearing written signs describing their offenses. I mention this Chinese example to highlight the cross-cultural appeal of sign shaming, as people in various regions of the world have been shamed using written signs—either held or hung around their necks—for hundreds of years. Shame parades of various kinds have recently gained renewed popularity in the United States, with people young and old being compelled by authority figures to suffer the embarrassment of standing in public holding a sign that describes the particulars of some wrongdoing.

When signs are used to publically humiliate and shame people, legal scholars call this a "shaming penalty." Such punishments have been debated in the legal literature, and Lauren Goldman has noted that "believing that public shaming punishments generally have the ability to positively affect their children's behavior, parents have utilized public shaming punishments in much the same way as courts have." When judges and parents mete out shaming punishments, the intention is not to produce the same kind of amusing, lighthearted effect found in the dog-shaming photographs. Instead, when people are made to hold or wear written signs in public, the goal is almost always to create a real and potentially transformative sense of social anguish that comes from being associated with an embarrassing message that has been crafted by someone else. "I am a clown. I speak Spanish," read Cesar Chavez's sign.[2]

In this chapter, I explore the curious, long-standing, and widespread theater of having people hold or wear written signs in public to shame them. Like writing a student's name on the chalkboard, which I discussed in the previous chapter, this is a way that writing is used to call people out in public, and through sociorhetorical pressure try to control, shame, and (potentially) curb deviant behavior. While most of the forms of writing as punishment used in schools attempt to use the *act of writing* to transform the punished person, this form of writing-based punishment does not require any actual writing on behalf of the person being punished. Instead, this punishment attempts to forge a link between a written message and the person associated with it. This dynamic of transposed authorship is embedded in a power relationship in which a disempowered speaker (the sign holder) is made to express the words of another author or ghost writer (the judge or parent). The written sign, in a sense, represents and makes this power relationship possible. Said another way, writing has the ability to foster and solidify such power relations.

The signs people hold in the scenes I describe call out the sign holder, much like a teacher writing a name on a chalkboard, and shaming signs accomplish their form of discipline by involving a sign-reading public.

Often, the message on the sign is one of regret; in other cases, the sign details the crime or offense and tries to foster public scorn. The identities of sign holders, while they are being punished by holding or wearing a written sign in public, are temporarily reduced to the static messages that they are made to hold. Ultimately, the job of writing in these scenes of public shaming is to try to make fools of a particular kind: this kind of writing-based punishment creates sign holders who are deprived of their literate authority and reduced to a simple message of admission written by someone else.

In shame parades, power and authority are established and symbolized through the use of signs that act as mandated speech, which can be thought of as the antithesis of free speech.[3] If free speech is the right to express what one chooses without limit or censorship, mandated speech involves compelling someone to express a message against his or her will. In shame parades, holding or wearing the sign symbolizes that the person being shamed has submitted to having his or her free expression regulated or supplanted via writing. Writing is literally held up as a sanctioned way to take free speech away, if only for the duration of the sign shaming. Shame parades use writing to manufacture and celebrate authority through submission to the words on the sign, and running through shame parades is a sense that the shamers and onlookers derive some kind of satisfaction from the theatrical scene of public humiliation. Writing about the popularity of humiliation in contemporary culture, Wayne Koestenbaum observes that humiliation often involves a triangle of participants—"tyrant, victim, [and] witness"—and is often arousing to some or all members involved. In shame parades, writing makes all of this happen.[4]

In the public shamings I discuss from the contemporary US context, judges and parents orchestrate the shame parades. Parents are relatively new to the scene of this kind of public punishment, but as I describe, judges and other public officials have long required such signs. These sign shamings actively draw upon a legacy of the public pillory, where punishment was accomplished via symbolic acts of various kinds in a public scene, and the power they work to leverage is embedded in the feeling of shame itself. In a discussion about shame and the body, Catherine Olive-Marie Fox writes that "in shame our very sense of self is made questionable. It taps into our sense of identity: more than an act or behavior, it speaks to who we are." Shame parades attempt to question this sense of self.[5]

To explore the use of writing in these particular forms of public shaming, I begin with two historically distant examples of sign shaming in public. These examples show some of the origins of this kind of public shaming, as well as just how extreme shame parades can be. I then shift the focus to two contemporary varieties of sign shaming: instances where judges have required that signs be held up in public and instances where parents have compelled their children to hold signs on roadsides and on social media. In the conclusion to this chapter, I describe how these scenes amount to preconditioned degradation ceremonies that rely on the signs to foster (potentially) transformative shame.

In all of these cases, writing is taken up and used to punish and shame because it is seen not as an enriching communication tool or a particularly wonderful vehicle for self-expression but because writing is perceived as a useful instrument for enacting justice through rhetorical social action.

HISTORY

In 1625, an Italian woman "was convicted on nine counts of having performed 'sorcery, magic, and diabolical operations'" and made to spend "one hour locked in the stocks in San Marco with a sign around her neck saying 'For Witchcraft,'" before being sent to prison. The sign clarified the nature of the woman's crime and figuratively branded her a witch. But not all sign shamings are part of sentences passed down by a judge. Flash forward to Peru in the 1980s, where a group of women took action against a known domestic abuser, stripping "him naked and [hanging] a sign around his neck saying, 'I will never abuse my wife again.'" In what follows, I discuss how punishment signs were used in two very distant historical contexts: colonial America in the 1600s and Nazi Germany in the 1930s. While these situations are far from one another and distant from the present-day United States, considering how written signs were used in both contexts questions the presumption that contemporary shame parades are merely trivial and harmless. The colonial American and Nazi examples show the extreme potentials of shame parades.[6]

Colonial America

Historians agree that the legal punishments in colonial America were often harsh, conducted in public, and informed by religious precepts. Punishments such as branding, whipping, ducking (dunking a person in water while he or she was strapped to a chair), and being locked in the stocks were not uncommon. In some cases, those who were locked in a public pillory would have one ear nailed to the wooden post; when the person was released, all or part of the ear would tear free, leaving a permanent reminder of the crime.[7] Amid all this blood and gore, historians have documented the use of written signs in punishments in the American colonies in 1600s. Such signs functioned as a legible reminder of a person's crime and, importantly, sinful nature.

Laura Bufano Edge, in her history of punishment in America, notes that "a woman who skipped a church service might be forced to stand in front of the church with a large sign around her neck to announce her sin." The sign put a label on the criminal, simplifying and publicizing the offense. In 1672, when Sarah Roe was convicted of "unlawful familiarity"—the puritanical way of describing adultery—she was jailed and "ordered to appear before congregants in the Ipswich meetinghouse wearing a sign that read 'FOR MY BAUDISH CARRIAGE.'" In this case, a written sign singled her out and unequivocally associated Sarah Roe with what was seen as, at the time, an unspeakable crime. Speaking the unspeakable is one key function of written signs in public shamings: the sign reduces the person's ability to represent him- or herself while transforming a complex individual into a single, shameful message.[8]

But the most well-known use of writing to produce shame during the American colonial period was popularized by Nathaniel Hawthorne in his novel *The Scarlet Letter*, set in the 1640s. In the 1850 novel, the character Hester Prynne is made to wear a scarlet letter *A* on her clothing to express to her community that she has committed adultery. Scholars have debated whether or not Hawthorne based *The Scarlet Letter* on a real-life case, but Hawthorne scholar Joel Berson settles the issue in his detailed account of the laws and punishment practices in the colonies in the 1600s. Berson writes that "the Plymouth law prescribing the wearing of the letters AD upon conviction for adultery was enacted in 1658, somewhat after the period of *The Scarlet Letter*." Even before this law of 1658 was passed, Berson notes that such letters were frequently required by judges. Much like the practice of branding criminals with a single letter to symbolize their crime, signifying letters were sometimes affixed to the garments of those found guilty of crimes.[9]

So, in the colonial context in North America, forms of writing-based punishments established social stigma, degradation, and shame. This was intensified in Nazi Germany, which I discuss next, where writing-based punishments dehumanized and helped fuel discrimination.

Nazi Germany
Many forms of public shaming and ridicule were used during the Nazi era, with written signs being just one way that targeted groups were humiliated and singled out in public. As the Nazis began to take power of

Germany in 1933, signs reading "Jew" and "Jewish" were placed on businesses and in neighborhoods to mark owners and occupants. Signs were also used to ridicule and stigmatize individuals who were paraded in public. For instance, in 1935, a group of Jewish business owners were made to walk through the streets of Leipzig carrying signs that read, "Don't buy from Jews. Shop in German businesses."[10] These signs did more than make Jews promote Nazi policies; parading the signs in public manufactured public displays of submission and signaled how written language could become a dangerous tool wielded by a literate regime.

People who the Nazis wanted to shame, ridicule, and make examples of were paraded through major German cities holding a variety of written signs. A well-known instance of this sign shaming involved Jewish lawyer Michael Siegel, who, in 1933, was ridiculed and punished for asking the police for assistance. Siegel was shaved bald, his pants were cut short, and he was marched barefoot through the streets of Munich holding a sign that read, "I will never complain to the police again" (Ich werde mich nie mehr bei der Polizei beschweren) (fig. 2.2).[11] Most accounts of this public shaming place the responsibility on the Sturmabteilung, or Stormtroopers.

Similarly, people deemed to be "Jewish sympathizers" were subjected to their own shame parades. Figure 2.3 depicts an incident in which a German woman was made to wear a sign that read, "I am the biggest pig in town and get involved only with *Jews*!" (Ich bin am Ort das größte Schwein und lass mich nur mit *Juden* ein!) The man in the image holds a sign that reads, "As a Jewish boy, I *always* take only German girls up to my room!" (Ich nehm als Judenjunge *immer* nur deutsche Mädchen mit aufs Zimmer!)[12] In shame parades, the content of the written signs is intended to shame and humiliate—but regardless of what the sign says, being made to

Figure 2.2. Michael Siegel in 1933 being made to walk through Munich holding a written sign that reads, "I will never complain to the police again" (Ich werde mich nie mehr bei der Polizei beschweren).

Figure 2.3. A woman and man accused of being Jewish sympathizers are made to wear written signs in public. Her sign reads, "I am the biggest pig in town and get involved only with *Jews*!" (Ich bin am Ort das größte Schwein und lass mich nur mit *Juden* ein!) His sign reads, "As a Jewish boy, I *always* take only German girls up to my room!" (Ich nehm als Judenjunge *immer* nur deutsche Mädchen mit aufs Zimmer!)

hold such a message in public singles the person out and diminishes his or her power of self-representation.

As Jürgen Matthäus and Mark Roseman write in their book *Jewish Responses to Persecution: 1933–1938*, "an Aryan caught buying in a Jewish store was often made to walk the streets wearing a large placard" that read, "I am a German swine and buy at Jewish shops." Anyone could be targeted for public shaming with these signs. Drunks, for instance, were sometimes made to march through city streets with shameful signs reading, "I have drunk away the whole of my wages." These are scenes in which written language is weaponized by the state to affix condemnatory labels to all kinds to citizens. In the broadest sense, writing is construed through such shame parades as a normative force.[13]

It is worth considering these examples of public shaming, from colonial America and Nazi Germany, for several reasons. The first is simply to keep in mind that shame parades are not new. Writing has long been used in punishments of this kind to mark individuals, force them to express ideas against their will, and reduce the punished to the words written on a sign. The sustained popularity of this form of punishment has come from and helped to maintain an undercurrent of assumptions about writing as a tool that can dominate, control, overpower, and transform us. Writing, as demonstrated in shame parades, is to be feared.

In addition, these examples remind us that shame parades simply cannot be assessed across time and place as having any single kind of significance or level of humaneness and/or cruelty. This is why I began this chapter with the example of dog shaming: what is funny and cute in one situation (e.g., dog shaming) can be seen as unbearably cruel in another (e.g., Nazi shame parades). Punishments involving written signs have been carried out in different cultural contexts to produce different intensities of public shame. There are big differences between what it meant for Sarah Roe to wear a sign that read "FOR MY BAUDISH CARRIAGE" in 1672 and for Michael Siegel to be marched through the streets of Munich wearing a sign in 1933. Each experience was surely intense for the wearer of the sign, but each cultural context made the intensity and meaning of the experience distinct. With that said, there is a bottom line here: this form of punishment has consistently relied on written signs to act as mandated speech imposed on the person being punished.

And lastly, it is important to keep these historical examples in mind because past uses of written signs to produce public shame have not always been as seemingly benign as today's uses of written signs appear to be. In the contemporary cases I describe, signs are used to shame and humiliate people in public, but it is hard to characterize them as downright cruel, abusive, and inhumane in the way that Nazi shame parades were. The use of written signs to produce shame in Nazi Germany appears to us, now, as deeply sadistic and cruel. Knowing what we now know about the Nazi regime, these public punishments look to be one small step toward the larger mission of isolating, condemning, and ultimately exterminating the Jews. I cannot help but wonder if we have become so inured to our contemporary culture of punishment that we cannot fully see the intensity with which people are being punished in public. Said another way, sign shaming has been reintroduced as normal and benign in our time, but these historical examples show just how extreme it can be.

THE JUDGE MADE ME SAY IT

In a law review article from 1999 on the topic of "modern shame punishment," Aaron S. Book writes that "frustrated with the ineffectiveness of traditional forms of punishment, judges are imposing sentences of shame upon convicted criminals more frequently."[14] Sixteen years after this observation, such sentences continue to be issued in US courts. Municipalities post mug shots online, pictures of convicted criminals can be seen on public billboards, and sex offenders can be identified via signs in their front yards and pins on online maps. Calling out the convicted by making them stand in public holding signs scrawled with court-mandated messages is part of a larger trend of publically shaming the convicted.

In US law review journals, the efficacy, legality, and morality of shame-based punishments have been hotly debated. Dan Kahan, perhaps the biggest scholarly proponent of this sentencing approach, published both a 1999 University of Chicago law review article arguing for the efficacy of shame-based punishments *and* a later 2006 Yale law review piece renouncing his previous position. With Kahan's renunciation, shaming punishments may have lost their biggest scholarly supporter, but the outcome of *United States v. Gementera* put shame-based sentences on solid legal ground. In the case, Shawn Gementera was convicted of stealing mail in San Francisco and made to wear a signboard at the post office that read, "I stole mail. This is my punishment." His attorneys argued that the humiliating punishment was unjust, but the court found otherwise. The court documents read: "While humiliation may well be—indeed likely will be—a feature of defendant's experience in standing before a post office with such a sign, the humiliation or shame he experiences should serve the salutary purpose of bringing defendant in close touch with the real significance of the crime he has acknowledged committing." With sign shaming found by the court to have a "legitimate statutory purpose of rehabilitation," scholars such as Lauren Goldman have argued that court-ordered public shaming should expand to the Internet and social media spaces.[15]

But shame-based punishments still have their detractors. As Martha Nussbaum puts it in a scathing critique of shame-based legal punishments, "a decent society, one might think, would treat its citizens with respect for their human dignity, rather than degrading or humiliating them." Nussbaum synthesizes existing legal scholarship on shame-based punishments, finding five main oppositions to such sentences in the literature: shaming the convicted is an offense against human dignity, based on mob justice, proven to be unreliable, a lousy deterrent, and part of a troubling and "ever-widening attempt to put more people under social control." Jurisprudence, or the theory and philosophy of law, does not always govern what happens in US courts—so some judges continue to issue shame-based sentences.[16]

Here is a sampling of recent court-ordered, shame-based punishments involving sign-shaming: In 2014, an Ohio man was convicted of disorderly conduct and harassing his neighbors. The judge sentenced him to jail time, probation, community service, and time holding a sign alongside a busy road. For five hours, the man was made to hold a sign that read, "I am a bully. I pick on children that are disabled and I am intolerant of those that are different from myself. My actions do not reflect an appreciation for the diverse south Euclid community that I live in" (fig. 2.4). This case was not unusual, as an array of adults have been sentenced to hold written signs in public in recent years. In another case in Ohio, this one in 2012 and overseen by a different judge, a woman who drove on a sidewalk to get around a stopped school bus was made to stand on a street corner holding a sign that read, "Only an idiot would drive on the sidewalk to avoid a school bus." In another case, a woman had to hold a sign that read, "I stole from a local merchant." In yet another case, the sign read, "I stole from a 9 year old on her birthday! Don't steal or this could happen to you!" In some of these cases, jail time was avoided or lessened when the defendant consented to be part of a shame parade.[17]

In this age of online social media, when shameful and embarrassing images can go viral on the Internet in very little time, making someone hold up a cardboard sign in public may seem antiquated or ineffective. A hundred people might see the person holding the sign on a street corner, whereas thousands can see an embarrassing photo on Instagram or Facebook in a single day. But the purpose of the shame parade is not just to get maximum exposure; holding the sign is meant to immediately and publicly humiliate. As Koestenbaum writes, humiliation has "the potential . . . to transfigure the person over whom it casts a noxious cloud."[18] Shame parades are rhetorical scenes, akin to writing a student's name on the chalkboard in a classroom, that are crafted to involve onlookers in the production of shame while tapping into the tradition of the public pillory—and by doing so, they construe writing as an integral tool used by the justice system to maintain social control.

A simple handwritten message, held up in public, transposes authorship onto the convicted and mandates certain speech before witnesses. Shame parades minimize the rhetorical agency of the person on parade, as his or her expressive potential is largely usurped, if only during the parade, to what is written on the sign. And the inferred value placed on writing is that it can be used against you. With the sign as a focal point for onlookers, shame parades even manage to temper or suspend the coveted right of free speech, reducing one's right to free and unlimited expression as the sign bearer promotes an imposed message. The First Amendment states that "Congress shall make no law . . . abridging the freedom of speech," but shame parades at least temporarily infringe on free speech by requiring the person who is punished to hold up a court-mandated message.[19] Shame parades use simple written signs to celebrate powers of the state to require citizens to say, in writing, what the court determines.

Each time holding or wearing a written sign is mandated in this way, a case is publically made for the transformative potential of public written discourse. Brief, written statements held up in public spaces are represented by the judges who institute such shame parades as capable of labeling an individual and making that person a target for socially productive public scorn. Writing can transform the people on parade, these theatrical uses of writing insist, as writing can speak for you and be imposed on you. Writing

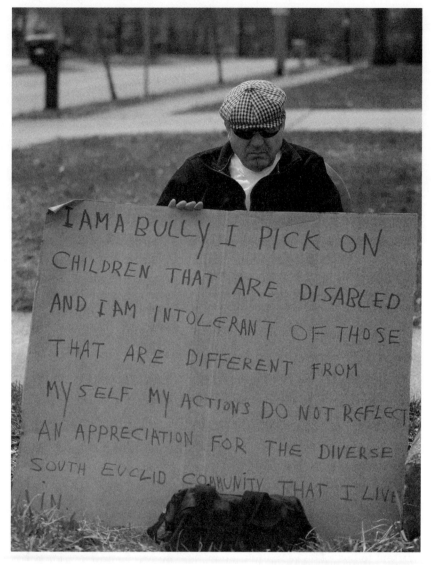

Figure 2.4. Man made to hold an antibullying and antidiscrimination sign after being convicted of harassing his neighbors in Ohio in 2014. © 2014 Associated Press.

is also represented as potentially dangerous because it can ostensibly be used to publically tell the truth about you. And writing symbolizes a person has submitted, at least temporarily, to a narrative created by the state. In an even more basic sense, shame parades come from and perpetuate an authoritative belief in the power and truth of the written word. Writing, these court sentences advertise to onlookers, can be wielded by the state and should be feared.

MY PARENT MADE ME SAY IT

Not only judges feel authorized to institute shame parades. In recent years, the media has reported on a number of cases in the United States in which parents have made their children display written signs in public—on city streets, near schools, and online. In these cases, parents have acted independently, instituting shame parades as forms of parental discipline. As Lauren Goldman puts it, "believing that public shaming punishments generally have the ability to positively affect their children's behavior, parents have utilized public shaming punishments in much the same way as courts have."[20]

Take Donnell Bryant for example. In 2012, he made his ninth-grade daughter walk alongside a North Carolina highway holding a sign that read, "I have a bad attitude. I disrespect people who try to help me." The back of the sign read, "I do what I want, when I want, how I want." In 2012, a teenager in Florida was made to stand beside a large plywood sign that had her name on top and read: "I sneak boys in at 3 A.M. and disrespect my parents and grandparents." The written signs used in these punishments often frame the kids as suffering from a lack of respect for their parents. And in some media reports of these parent-mandated shame parades, one or both parents assert their authority by standing alongside their child, who is holding the sign.[21]

Perhaps ironically, since sign shaming relies on public humiliation, many of these signs focus on bullying. In California in 2007, a seventh grader was suspended from school for bullying, and during her suspension, her mother made her stand in front of area schools holding a sign that read, "I engaged in bullying behavior. I Got Suspended from school and this street corner. Don't be like me. STOP BULLYING." In 2013, a Texas fourth-grader was made to hold a sign that told passersby, "I AM A BULLY. *Honk*! if you hate bullies." In Miami, another child was seen with a sign that read, "I was sent to School, to get an Education. NOT to be a BULLY. . . . I was Not Raised THIS WAY!!!!!" These shame parades fall into the trap of enacting the very thing they critique: forcing a child to hold an embarrassing sign in public is, if not identical to bullying, at least closely aligned with it. Both bullying and shame parades thrive on shame and humiliation. But child shaming of this kind is rendered somehow okay and socially acceptable through the logic of the shame parade.[22]

By putting children through a shame parade, the parents who use this punishment elicit public endorsement for their approach to discipline, values, and beliefs. At a busy intersection in Miami in 2012, the value was good grades when a boy was made to hold a sign that read, "Hey I want to be a class clown. Is it wrong?" The other side of the sign read: "I'm in the seventh grade and got three Fs. Blow your horn if there's something wrong with that." The boy's father stood beside him during the punishment, and with passing cars occasionally honking, the father told a reporter that the punishment was a "last resort" to help his son. In 2007, a North Carolina teenager was made to hold a sign in public that read, "I steal from my family." An Illinois eight-year-old watched cars go by while wearing a handmade sign that said, "I like to steal from others and lie about it!!" Another child's sign said, "I was disrespecting my parents by twerking at my school dance." Yes, twerking. Unlike signs imposed by judges, which generally refer to broken laws, parents who choose this form of punishment use written signs to address broken family rules and disregarded values, seeking support from a larger community via the scene of public punishment.[23]

Parents interested in shaming their children in public have not limited themselves to city streets and public highways. Some parents have taken to the Internet to display images of their children holding signs scrawled with an array of embarrassing messages. In Ohio in 2012, for instance, a mother changed her daughter's Facebook profile picture to an image of the girl superimposed with text that read: "I do not know how to keep my [mouth shut]. I am no longer allowed on Facebook or my phone. Please ask why. My Mom says I have to answer everyone who asks." In a similar online public shaming that was posted to social media, a young girl was shown holding a handwritten sign that read, "My name is Hailey. I am a kind, caring, smart girl, but I make poor choices with social media." The detailed sign goes on to say that the girl will be selling her iPod (featured in the image) and donating the money to an antibullying charity. In 2012, a Houston mother made her daughter post a picture of herself holding a sign that read, "Since I want to post photos of me holding liquor, I am obviously *not* ready for social media and will be taking a hiatus until I learn what I should and should not post! Bye-Bye." The image circulated widely after being posted to Facebook and Instagram. These are web 2.0 versions of shame parades.[24]

Parents who compel their children to hold written signs in public—both on street corners and in photos posted online—mandate that the children express and become associated with disquieting messages. In addition, the punishments indirectly insist that simple forms of written language can be used as a tool, wielded by adults and used to control children. Even online, where Photoshopped and highly designed images are commonplace, social media sign shamings involve children being made to hold rudimentary, handwritten signs replete with grammatical errors and juvenile handwriting. The simplicity of these online sign-shaming images refers to shame parades held on city streets, reemphasizing the notion that even the most fundamentally constructed written texts can be consequential. The parents who orchestrate these shamings also exert a type of judge-like, or extrajudicial, public authority over their children, in some cases standing beside the child to emphasize the parent's role in making the shame parade happen.

Giving the parents who have used this kind of punishment the benefit of the doubt, let's assume for a moment that parents who punish their children in this way are motivated by only the best intentions. They want to shape, teach, and raise their children in the best possible ways, and they are using publically displayed writing to do so. While it would be impossible to know all of the motives behind these punishments, I am comfortable concluding that there are at least three basic goals at work here: having children hold up written signs as punishment (1) exerts authority and power over the children, (2) disrupts the familiar flow of everyday life for the kids, and (3) tries to publicize what the children did wrong. These three goals are not only relevant to the public shaming of children but to the contemporary uses of written signs as punishment more generally. It also says a great deal about how we view writing.

Note that of these three goals, a written sign is only really essential in the accomplishment of the third goal, making actions public, and it is certainly not the only way to achieve that publicity. Parents, like judges, can exert their authority, disrupt the flow of everyday life, and publicize their children's actions without a handmade written sign. So why, in the second decade of the twenty-first century, are children being made to stand on street corners and before their friends on social media holding signs describing themselves as bullies, thieves, bad students, and disrespectful adolescents? Why is writing used in these scenes of public shame?

For me, the main answers lie in how accustomed we are to thinking of writing-based punishments as forward-thinking, benign, and civilized. Making a person hold up a sign in public demands some degree of submission from the sign holder, and getting complete submission from children can be appealing to some parents. These public shamings force admissions of guilt—"I am a bully" or "I steal from my family"—and extend those admissions over a period of time for a public to witness. The power of the scene is compounded by taking place in public. Public shamings involving written signs require the person being punished not only to implicate themselves in the act of wrongdoing but to stand up in public making that implication via a self-effacing statement for a period of time. And judging from the expressions on some of these children's faces, holding one of these signs looks pretty excruciating.

It is also important to think about what it means that some parents have moved this form of punishment into online spaces. Online public shamings of children may remove the physical experience of holding a sign in public, but online shame parades quickly tap into the child's immediate and potentially large social network. Mandated speech in online venues such as Facebook or Instagram is qualitatively different from forcing a child to hold a sign in public in that few children want to hold up *any* sign stating *anything* on a street corner, whereas many kids do have social media accounts and desire control over their self-expression in online worlds. Online, many children have a lot to say. On social media, many of us work hard to determine the messages that are available about ourselves—and children are no exception. The parents who punish and shame their kids online take this powerful form of self-expression away, mandating self-effacing representations via the very old technology of the shame parade.

THE DEGRADATION OF WRITING

There are many reasons to hold up a written sign in public. Some are courageous: maybe you are one of the many people who, in 2014, held up signs that read "Black Lives Matter." Or you could be Juan Mann (a pseudonym), the Australian man who became known in the early 2000s for holding a sign that read "FREE HUGS." Juan Mann's sign and his hugs started a global campaign promoting random acts of kindness. Or you could be an antiwar protestor holding up a sign demanding an end to a violent conflict. You could even be holding a sign that reads "Homeless, Please Help" in an effort to feed your family and indirectly protest the failing social safety net. These signs do not necessarily shame their holders but try to bring about material changes in the world.

And other handheld signs are relatively inconsequential. think of the signs drivers hold up at airports bearing the last names of their passengers or signs held up at sporting events promoting a favorite team. These signs get things done without aiming to thoroughly transform the world. In today's media landscape of ubiquitous electronic communication, old-fashioned, handwritten signs remain a salient form of communication helping people accomplish things with writing.

The signs discussed in this chapter are neither heroic nor mundane in that they are displayed involuntarily in a sort of street theater: the sign bearer is made to perform a punishment before an audience of passersby. It can be helpful to think of these shame parades as degradation ceremonies. Writing in the 1950s, American sociologist Harold Garfinkel argued that degradation ceremonies are integral to most societies. Garfinkel writes: "In our society the arena of degradation whose product, the redefined person, enjoys the widest transferability between groups has been rationalized, at least as to the institutional measures for carrying it out. The court and its officers have something like a fair monopoly over such ceremonies, and there they have become an occupational routine."[25] What he is saying here is that degradation ceremonies of various kinds have become normal, and that it has increasingly become the case that judges and police officers set such ceremonies in motion. In shame parades, the state of degradation for the sign holder is created through the powers of a static, written message that aims to create shame in the individual and thus bring about personal transformation.

For the purposes of this book, this chapter brings up two separate but related questions about the use of written signs to shame people in public: (1) What are the cultural implications of this kind of punishment? And (2) what can we learn about writing from shame parades?

For me, the first question has a very simple and entirely unsatisfactory answer: it depends. Written signs have been used to shame people in widely different cultural contexts—from colonial America in the 1600s to Nazi Germany in the 1930s to the United States in the early 2000s—and all of these shame parades have had different cultural implications. Forcing lawyer Michael Siegel to walk through the streets of Munich in 1933 carrying a sign denouncing his actions as a Jew was not the same as making a child hold up a sign that reads, "I was disrespecting my parents by twerking at my school dance." But, it is also the case that these two shame parades, separated by nearly a hundred years, have some things in common. They establish forms of social control, and they leverage the humiliating potentials of mandating certain forms of speech. But the meanings and implications of individual shame parades depend on all the particulars of the cultural moments they occur in.

However, I think there are some much more concrete and satisfying answers to the second question: What can we learn about writing from shame parades? For me, it comes back to the dog-shaming images I started this chapter with. Recall that in those images, the dogs have no way of representing themselves or their actions; instead, the signs do all the work of telling each dog's presumed story of mischief and wrongdoing. The author of the sign is obviously not the dog, but the signs pretend to be confessions: "I ate the cushions" or "I peed on the potato chip bag." In these scenes, written language does not necessarily have authentic, verifiable links to what authors actually think and feel. Instead, a written text can be nothing more than what we were made to say. If I hold up or otherwise vouch for a piece of writing, it is not necessarily an expression of my ideas or personal rhetorical agency. The words you are reading may have been written by someone else, or required by that person, and I may not even believe them. A piece of writing, shame parades tell us, can be both untrue and disempowering.

Holding up a confessional sign is unusual. If we all walked around each day carrying signs confessing misdeeds, the punishments mentioned in this chapter would lose their power. But standing on the side of the road holding up a sign describing some wrongdoing draws attention. And if you are holding such a sign, it is safe to say that you are disempowered to the extent that someone with authority over you made you do it. The writing, in these cases, represents that power relationship.

So far in this book, my examples have focused on writing-based punishments meted out by teachers, judges, and parents in their roles as authority figures in the institutions of the school, court, and home. In the next two chapters, all of that changes. For a variety of reasons, people outside of these institutions also use writing to disempower others, shame them, and punish.

THREE

WRITING ON THE WASTED

Thanks for the cereal. By the way, it says "balls" on your face.
—Tim in the film *Garden State*

Imagine a party atmosphere: loud music, lots of people, and flowing alcohol. Now, imagine that some people at this party are eager for the thrill of getting the writing started. In a sense, this is how drunk shaming works, as partiers wait until someone passes out to start writing and drawing on them. Now imagine for a moment that you are the one who awakens the next morning to find yourself stripped half-naked and covered in anonymous writing. I do not think any of our reactions would be exactly the same if this happened to us, as our feelings would depend on so many things about ourselves and the situation—but suffice it to say that some of us would be completely mortified. As a vernacular form of writing, drunk shaming wields an exquisitely devious type of power as the shamers alter something many of us work to control and cultivate: our physical body and outward appearance.

In April 2013, news outlets began reporting on the tragic case of Audrie Pott, a fifteen-year-old California girl who passed out at a party, was sexually assaulted by several male teenagers, and later killed herself. As more details about the case were revealed, it turned out that writing played a curious role in the case: while Audrie Pott was unconscious, she was not only sexually assaulted, she was also written on. While drunk shaming does not always involve sexual assault, it does combine writing with violation as targets are temporarily overwritten with text without their consent.

The *Los Angeles Times* quoted the Pott's family attorney, Robert Allard, as saying "there were some markings on her body, in some sort of permanent marker, indicating that someone had violated her when she was sleeping." The *Times* went on to note that "On Audrie's leg was a message . . . that included a boy's name and the words 'was here.'" The UK's *Daily Mail* reported that "other humiliating messages and arrows were daubed across her body by the three Saratoga High School football players." Some months after the attack, *Rolling Stone* published a detailed account of the incident titled "Sexting, Shame and Suicide: A Shocking Tale of Sexual Assault in the Digital Age." In the article, Pott's attackers were also described as having written the word "'anal' above her ass with an arrow pointing down." Robert Salonga, of the San Jose *Mercury News*, reported that Audrie Pott took her own life after learning that images taken of her during the attack had been circulated around her high school.[1]

Audrie Pott's is not the only recent case of drunk shaming that resulted in serious consequences. In several high-profile cases in the United States, young people have passed out, been drunk shamed, and later died from alcohol poisoning. When University of Colorado freshman Gordie Bailey died of an alcohol overdose in 2004, the coroner's report indicated that he had such things written on him as "It sucks to be you" and the word "Bitch." At the University of Texas, freshman Phanta Phoummarath died from an alcohol overdose at a party, and the "medical examiner's office reported that partygoers had used green and black markers to write 'FAG,' 'I'm gay' and 'I AM FAT' on Phoummarath's head, face, torso, legs and feet." There is no shortage of court cases indicating that the party game of drunk shaming can even take place when someone needs serious medical assistance.[2]

So it is clear that Audrie Pott's attackers did not spontaneously come up with the idea of writing on their unconscious victim. Even what they wrote—including the word "anal" on her lower back—reflected familiar ways that female victims of drunk shaming are also slut shamed. By transforming Audrie Pott's skin into a sort of muddled and incomplete written transcript of what happened the night before, the teenagers participated in an established form of vernacular writing. I describe drunk shaming in this way because writing on someone who has fallen unconscious is not really formalized or consistently practiced, and it is certainly not taught in schools or even recognized by many as a writing form. And yet, it is widespread, has been around for several decades, is celebrated in viral images online, and has been represented in some contemporary films and videos as nothing more than a humorous cultural commonplace. Those who write on people who have passed out drunk do not learn this kind of writing in a language arts class, style guide, or writing handbook. But drunk shaming is a socially acquired ritual and writing practice with conventions and shared practices much like other vernacular writing practices such as writing on restroom walls or writing on somebody's cast.

In restroom graffiti, authors largely remain anonymous, the writing can be offensive, and there are gendered dynamics to what gets written in men's and women's restrooms. A key difference between restroom graffiti writing and drunk shaming is that restroom graffiti does not come about through a nonconsensual violation of the physical body. In the ritual of drunk shaming, the victim's physical space and body are violated, and the writing that results is a kind of dangerous and salacious form of nonconsensual speech. In a very different context, take a medical office for instance, informed consent would be required before any invasive procedure. As Vibhav Mithal puts it, "the roots of the doctrine of informed consent are found in the principle of bodily autonomy which implies that a patient shall have the exclusive right of self-determination as to what shall be done with his body." Drunk-shaming scenes are anything but consensual, as bodily autonomy is forsaken and victims wake up to find they are literally wearing graffiti.[3]

In cast writing, if a young person breaks a bone and has to wear a plaster cast, it might get written and drawn on. The written and drawn messages on the cast may include signatures, mottos, images, and more recently even hashtags. But note that casts are typically written on by known authors and with the consent of the person with the cast, and it is this consensual writing that gets worn on the body via the cast. Legal scholars call this level of voluntary participation "affirmative consent."[4] Drunk-shaming texts are not nearly as durable and long-lasting as those found in cast writing, and that is a good thing, as drunk-shaming texts are typically anonymous, nonconsensual, and graphic. So drunk shaming is not alone in being a form of vernacular writing, and it shares a good deal with the writing that happens on restroom walls and plaster casts. But what sets drunk shaming apart from these other vernacular writing practices is that drunk shaming is nonconsensual, anonymous writing on the body that is all about fostering humiliation, shame, ridicule, and discomfort for the target who gets physically written on.

It is worth noting that this vernacular writing form that I am calling *drunk shaming* is not even formalized enough to have an agreed-upon name. I use the term *drunk shaming* because that is how many of the images and videos of people who have been written on in these ways are tagged and labeled online, but the authors of *The Party Bible* refer to it as "chiefing," and in the UK getting written on while passed out is part of a party game called "drunk buckaroo" or "drunk human buckaroo."[5] In my own discussions about drunk shaming with undergraduates on the college campus where I teach, most of the students I have spoken with say that they did not know this kind of writing even had a name. And yet, they were all familiar with the practice. No matter the name or namelessness of it, drunk shaming uses writing to make fun of, label, shame, mark, and humiliate people in the very public space of a party and—because it is often done with pens and semipermanent markers—into the next day. What makes drunk shaming unique in comparison to the other writing-based punishment and degradation rituals described in this book is that here authors write on a person's body without their knowledge or consent in a social atmosphere of wanton drunkenness.

Drunk shaming has many layers of meaning to it when examined as a writing practice. It overwrites someone's body with new kinds of legible meaning—if only temporarily—using words, symbols, and objects that label and call attention to the victim of the event. In this way, drunk shaming has several things in common with sign shaming via shame parades (discussed in chapter 2), except that in sign shaming, a person is required to and often consents to hold a sign in public. Like sign shaming, drunk shaming relies on the rhetorical logic of transposed authorship in that the shamers impose divisive words and images on to a victim who then has to "wear" and represent what is written. A key difference, however, is that drunk shaming typically involves a treacherous mix of erotic and despicable speech, creating bodies that are painfully uncomfortable to inhabit. In drunk shaming, the sign is the body of the target or victim, and the passed-out person is an unwilling participant. Note that drunk shaming also involves a group of average citizens carrying out the imposition, whereas authorities and people in power, such as judges and parents, carry out sign shaming. In drunk shaming, partiers become writers who violate and symbolically possess someone else, if only temporarily, through writing and drawing on their body. And what is created on the skin in drunk-shaming episodes resonates through multiple audiences: the first is present at the event, a second includes those who might read what was written the next day, and then still others may view images or video of the event online where hundreds of images from drunk shamings circulate on dedicated drunk-shaming websites. And all of this happens in what amounts to a party game. It is almost unfathomable to think of going up to a conscious friend or acquaintance and, without that person's consent, writing something on his or her face. And yet, in drunk shaming, this is exactly what happens—drunk shaming is a momentary suspension of everyday norms and taboos about bodily violation and writing. Drunk shaming involves a level of surprise and violation that is distinctly powerful.

This chapter approaches drunk shaming from a variety of perspectives. I rely on Tim Delaney's study of drunk shaming, which is described in his book *Shameful Behaviors*. I have also pored over various studies of college drinking more generally, as well as a variety of campus policies on drinking and drunkenness. I have gleaned some useful information about drunk shaming from an array of how-to-party books (yes, these books exist), and I have found some of the most revealing representations of drunk shaming online, both in photo and video form. I have also examined the few instances of drunk shaming represented in films and music videos. And lastly, in 2015, I conducted a small study (based on focus-group interviews) of attitudes about drunk shaming on the college campus where I teach.[6] While not definitive in any way, I conducted these focus-group interviews to gain more insight into the practice from people who are closer to it than I am, and I present excerpts from these conversations throughout this chapter.

Through all of these perspectives on drunk shaming, I have come to see it as a vernacular form of shame-generating writing that is similar in many ways to the other uses of writing as punishment described in this book. Drunk shaming is a shaming practice orchestrated by a swarming crowd, not a punishment meted out by a teacher or judge, and as such it has much less top-down or one-dimensional power dynamics. As the result of a crowd acting out, drunk shaming involves people in a sense self-policing, much like the many mass public shamings that have been seen online in recent years. Hanne Detel refers to a host of recent instances of "cyber mobs" attacking those who have been seen as violating social norms, and Jon Ronson describes how a swarm against an offensive Twitter user can erupt in mere minutes.[7] Drunk-shaming writers, and I think it is productive to call them that, also act en masse and seem to be drawn to the thrill of actually writing on the body of the person they target. Writing on an incapacitated drunk person is at once transgressive, erotic, discriminatory, and (perceived by many as) funny. And as the cases of Audrie Pott and others reveal, it can happen in a potentially dangerous and even criminal scene. But drunk shaming continues to be perceived as culturally acceptable within the logic of the ritual.

DRUNK SHAMING IN PRACTICE AND POPULAR CULTURE

Libby Copeland describes drunk shaming matter of factly in a *Washington Post* article: "An individual who has drunk himself into a stupor is decorated with markers, makeup, food and, occasionally, furniture."[8] And Copeland is careful to point out that those who fall prey to drunk shamers are not only written on. While writing is just part of what happens in drunk shaming, it is the most legible and interpretable part of a drunk-shaming event. One of the undergraduate students I spoke with in my focus group interviews described drunk shaming succinctly: "It's more stacking a lot of shit on top of them and then drawing on them." Another student I spoke with explained the motive for drunk shaming this way: "Some people get off at embarrassing other people."

Judging from the name, drunk shaming, it might seem as if this social ritual is all about producing shame, but my research on drunk shaming has left me convinced that the ritual simultaneously shames and celebrates off-the-rails drunkenness. One of the undergraduates I spoke with said that he thought drunk shaming happens because "no one wants the party to end." When "the first person goes down" and others write on him or her, this is a way to "encourage the drinking to go on." By writing on the first person to fall unconscious, the other people at the party "use that person as a motivator to keep everyone else going." So motivations vary in this vernacular practice.

Drunk shaming has some generally agreed upon rules, with a lot of the same things being done to people in the ritual across time and place. Not every rule is known by everyone, but these are some of the common ways drunk shaming works: One rule stipulates that the first person who passes out gets written on, as drunk shaming is all about singling out weakness and vulnerability. And then there is "the shoe rule," which states that you are only besieged by the crowd if you pass out with your shoes on. The shoe rule might sound odd, but it follows a certain logic: passing out with your shoes on means that you did not *intend* to sleep it off and thus lost control. So taking one's shoes off before passing out can protect you from being shamed, at least in most cases, as can being the host of the party. In his study of drunk shaming and treatment of it as a degradation ceremony, Delaney found that party hosts can be safe from drunk shaming, as can those with a spouse present—unless the spouse gives permission for the shaming.[9]

In my conversations about drunk shaming with undergraduates on my campus, I learned that some believe that intense forms of drunk shaming would constitute "taking things to a bullying level": writing on someone's face, for instance, or using permanent marker, or uploading an image of a close friend to the Internet. The students I spoke with tended to agree that, when close friends are involved, drunk shaming should involve some degree of compassion and sympathy, as opposed to downright cruelty.

But rules are loosely interpreted and tend to vary, and in some contexts drunk shaming remains an anything-goes affair, with outlandish and wild modifications not only fair game but "part of the fun." In drunk shaming, faces and bodies can be written on, people can be stripped naked or even bound, and it is common to pile garbage and/or food stuffs on top of the unconscious person. In my conversations with undergraduates at the university where I teach, however, there was a consensus that the shamers tend to take into consideration such things as what the victim has planned for the next day and whether or not the victim/target is a man or a woman. The students I spoke with agreed that it was more serious to drunk shame a woman than a man.

In one widely circulated video of a drunk shaming in action (posted to the humor site break.com and also on YouTube), a young man who has passed out is drawn and written on then carried to a small pond, where he is placed on an inflatable raft and floated out into the water—all while unconscious. For Tim Delaney, drunk shaming forces "the victim to yield to the wishes of others who are in a position of authority."[10] As the video of the man who was floated out into the pond demonstrates, drunk shamings can be risky, and as I have already shown, are sometimes coupled with much more serious offenses and consequences. Drunk shaming is part drinking game, part prank, and the more outlandish the images and videos that are produced in the process, the more likely the event is to go viral online.

Uploading and sharing videos and/or photos of drunk shaming has become built into the practice. In some of these photos, only the person who has been written on and otherwise adorned appears. In other photos, the shamer/writer poses beside his or her incapacitated (and often half-naked or fully naked) victim in a pose reminiscent of the big-game hunter posing beside the prize. A simple Google image search using the phrase "drunk shaming" yields a massive haul of such images, which are hosted across the web, mostly without attribution or the names of those depicted, at image-hosting "humor" sites such as collegehumor.com, drunkantics. com, dailyhaha.com, dirtybutton.com, and passedoutphotos.com.[11] In the images, you see ostensibly unconscious young people covered in every imaginable form of writing, drawing, wigs, cigarettes, and an array of other things being used to orchestrate the prank.

In one study of undergraduate narratives about drinking, drunk shaming was described in this way: "They pass out, you draw stuff on them. The best one was [name removed]. He, uh, he got all drunk last year, passed out, and they drew a cat on his face, like whiskers and everything? And he woke up and he went back started partying again and he had no idea what happened to him, he's just having a good time and everyone just laughed at him, because he thinks he's all cool, because he thinks he's the center of attention and but he's got that stuff drawn all over his face." From this description, we can see that drunk shaming is used to draw attention to an individual, to (perhaps lightly) ridicule him or her, and participants often take it up as a kind of repeatable game that is integrated into other drinking rituals. A story told by one of the undergraduates I spoke with was similar: "I remember I woke up one morning. I blacked out and I had like a giant penis right here [pointing toward his back] and I didn't even know it was there until I went to the shower." Another student told me "I've had it done to me before. I see the aftermath and it's not that bad. It's funny. It's not something I take to heart." In Tim Delaney's study of drunk shaming, however, he found that "seventy-three percent of all drunk shaming victims wanted revenge after being victimized by a drunk shaming." Whether it is funny or serious or both, what happened at the party remains mysteriously encrypted in what is written on the body. What was written and/or drawn becomes a set of clues about the events from the night before.[12]

Drunk-shaming rituals have been going on since at least the 1980s when I personally witnessed them at high school parties. While no history of drunk shaming has been written, there are some telling depictions of it in popular culture. Zach Braff's 2004 film *Garden State* is one example, in that the film's main character, Andrew Largeman (played by Braff), passes out at a party and, unbeknownst to him, spends much of the following day

Figure 3.1. Still taken at the 0:19 second mark in the music video for "Saturday" by Rebecca Black. Online at https://www.youtube.com/watch?v=GVCzdpagXOQ.

with the word "BALLS" written across his forehead in large letters. This is both mildly humiliating for Largeman and humorous in the context of the film, capturing how drunk shaming often works to get a laugh out of viewers/onlookers at the expense of the person who is written on. The movie represents drunk shaming as nothing more than a form of light-hearted, somewhat absurd fun.

Drunk shaming plays a similarly humorous and harmless role in the more recent 2013 music video for the song "Saturday," performed by online phenomenon Rebecca Black. In the video, cool teenagers party hard, stay up late, dance into the night, and when one teenage boy passes out at a party, the words "FUN FUN FUN FUN" are written across his face. Importantly, someone records the drunk shaming with a cell phone while it is happening (fig. 3.1). The music video represents this kind of writing as something cool kids do and integral to the larger life of the party.

References to drunk shaming in print media became more regular after the 2004 release of *Garden State*. Tim Delaney's *Shameful Behaviors* is the most detailed study of drunk shaming to date, with a full-scale study of drunk shaming among undergraduate students comprising the centerpiece of the book. Throughout, Delaney explores drunk shaming from a sociological perspective, asserting that drunk shaming is a ritual and part of a larger trend in contemporary culture toward public shaming. Delaney's study is complemented by a small array of stories that have been published in newspapers, most notably the detailed article (mentioned above) in the *Washington Post* from 2005 by Libby Copeland. In this piece, Copeland explores the lighter side of drunk shaming while pointing out the general rules that apply in drunk shamings and some of the relationships between drunk shaming and other forms of public humiliation.

Drunk shaming has gotten the most exposure from shamers themselves. In 2006, the media website collegehumor.com (established in 1999) posted its first image of a drunk-shaming victim, and by 2008 other sites dedicated to images of drunk shaming—passedoutphotos.com and drunkantics.com—were online and hosting hundreds of such images. Searching the web for terms such as "drunk shaming," "drunk written on," or "passed out Sharpie" now yields more drunk-shaming images than can be viewed in a single sitting. Many of these images have been uploaded to sites such as passedoutphotos.com, drunkantics.com, holytaco.com, or the network of other sites that either redirect to or are housed at collegehumor.com. YouTube and other video hosting sites have many videos of drunk shamings that appear to have been filmed on the scene and in live action. In the videos that appear to be of live drunk shamings, revelers write, joke, draw on faces, and laugh some more. Dedicated drunk-shaming image hosting sites, along with social networking platforms such as Facebook, have become vast repositories for the growing evidence of both the popularity of drunk shaming and the misguided view that drunk shaming is nothing but fun.

In the UK, where the activity of piling things on someone who has passed out is called playing "drunk buckaroo," images referring to drunk shamings have even been used to sell products. PRO PLUS caffeine pills (a subsidiary of Bayer) released such an ad campaign in 2011, relying on images featuring young men who appear to have fallen asleep or passed out and then, unbeknownst to them, been extensively written and drawn on. In the caffeine pill ads, the sleeping college students in the images look as if they fell asleep while reading books (sometimes this is called sleep shaming), but the images are actually derived from ones in real-life drunk shaming episodes that can be readily found online. In one of the ads for the caffeine pills, a young man is covered in a drawn tuxedo on his seminaked body, and the drawn outfit is a near replica of a well-known drunk-shaming image that has circulated widely online.

In one study of college drinking culture, Thomas Workman makes the point that even the most dangerously self-destructive drinking activities remain appealing because the activities provide some kind of perceived meaning to the participants. Workman argues "that high-risk drinking behavior, regardless of its outcome, is constructed by the collegiate culture as a positive, functional activity. The task for [Workman's] study is to identify the signification that produces this interpretation of a potentially deadly activity."[13] I follow Workman's thinking in seeing drunk shaming as a revealing suspension of normal societal rules; by paying attention to this suspension of the typical processes of everyday life, we can learn that drunk shaming may be a drinking game, but it is also a writing game. Participants write, of all things, at these drinking parties because of the perceived degradation potential of writing.

The rhetorical ritual of drunk shaming, which involves a writer or writers composing a nonconsensual text on the body of the person being shamed, suggests that it is appealing (at least for some) to write directly on someone's body without their consent. This is dangerous writing that violates and breaks social taboos. Any transgressive thrill that comes from covering another person with writing is linked to the fact that most drunk shamings involve the creation of uncomfortable speech and images. The things that drunk shamers write and draw come from the depths of some of the more graphic cultural vocabularies. In addition, this writing on the body is a very literal way to transpose authorship from the writer(s) to the victim, who has to bear the text. Once drunk-shaming writing and drawing is placed on the body, the rhetorical logic has it that—much like with sign shaming—the text becomes attached to and associated with the person who has been written on. The person who has been drunk shamed becomes not the author of whatever has been written but its representative.

In an average day, you probably do not write on someone's face or help carry someone who is unconscious out to a pond to see if that person will swim when he or she wakes up. Engaging in drunk-shaming rituals involves the suspension of what is deemed acceptable, and to the extent that writing on the body of the victim is integral to this practice, writing is used to make bodies into living billboards that shame, humiliate, and make fun of the victim. As I now go on to describe, the actual things that tend to be written and drawn on the hapless victims of drunk-shaming incidents have a good deal in common, as they rely on shame to be created through disquieting, socially unacceptable forms of speech.

DANGEROUS SPEECH

I started this chapter with the case of Audrie Pott because, while drunk shaming is often portrayed as "fun" and "just a game," there are clear themes of sexism and bodily violation running through this kind of writing. Certainly not all victims of drunk shaming are sexually assaulted like Audrie Pott was or end up dead like Gordie Bailey and Phanta Phoummarath did, but to think of drunk shaming as nothing more than a harmless prank ignores the serious implications encrypted in the frequently written themes composed by the shamers. Instead of seeing drunk shaming as "fun," think of it for a moment as an instance of one or more people seizing an opportunity to take advantage of another helpless person by writing directly onto their body. Writing is the weapon of choice because it is seen as having the ability to enact a very legible kind of bodily violation. As I looked through ten, twenty, a hundred, or more of the accumulated images tagged "drunk shaming" online, I began to see some troubling patterns: this written record reveals incessantly repeated themes of homophobia, misogyny, sexual violation, and racism. At a party where someone passes out and gets written on, it is not poetry or kind phrases that are likely to be written on the flesh. It is not signatures, like those written on plaster casts. It is not humorous jokes or happy faces. Instead, it is most often degrading cultural symbols and signifiers that create a readable, embodied cloak of shame and embarrassment. In a twisted way, the so-called "fun" comes out of the ignominious words and images that are scrawled all over the body.

In short, not everyone who falls victim to the creative arts of the drunk shamers is adorned with relatively harmless drawn-on tuxedos and kitty-cat whiskers. Instead, as one student I spoke with at my university put it, "you pass out, you get a dick on your face. It's that simple." Many of the readily available online images of drunk-shaming events feature profane terms and images scrawled across faces, torsos, and other body parts—and frequently the person being written on has been stripped naked in the process of being shamed by a thrill-seeking community of writers.

The most graphic images of drunk shaming reveal drunk-shaming writers working in the realm of discomfort, in that the texts they create, leave behind, and often photograph are anything but examples of civil discourse. A swastika, the word "ENTER" with an arrow pointing toward the victim's backside, the word "loser" and the phrase "fuck me"—these are commonplaces in drunk shaming. Drawings of penises, along with words such as "gay" and "fag," function in cultures based on heteronormativity to produce shame and discomfort. Drunk shamers tend to pull from a stock collection of offensive images, words, and expressions. Creating a highly volatile and offensive bodily text could be said to be the goal of the drunk-shaming author(s), and what gets written and drawn points to a shared system of beliefs about what is seen as most socially objectionable, bad, humiliating, and shameful. What remains unclear is whether the things being written are intended to be seen as the expressed views and opinions of those doing the writing or the person being written on or both. Drunk shaming leaves that up to the viewer to determine, but one thing is clear: the person being shamed is often left wearing, on his or her skin, a very disquieting litany of phrases and expressions.

And when women come under the pen, they are often slut shamed by having penises or the word "slut" drawn on them. In more conventional forms of slut shaming, which are widespread in the United States, girls and women are attacked and maligned for aspects of their appearance and/ or "presumed sexual activity."[14] A double bind informs slut shaming in that it both encourages women to be sexually desirable and discourages them from being sexually active, and a double standard is at work in that men are typically celebrated for sexual prowess while women are shamed for their sexuality. In scenes of drunk shaming that involve slut shaming, there is an additionally vexing dynamic at work in that the girls and women who are targets of drunk shaming are transformed, via the drawing and writing on their bodies, into the fictitiously "loose" or sexualized women, who can then be slut shamed. Female victims become particularly sought after targets of slut shaming when they are unconscious and vulnerable. The images and words that are drawn on the passed-out victim—things like penises and the word *slut*—manufacture the very stigmas that slut shaming critiques.

Keep in mind that while many targets of drunk shamings are written and drawn on, they are also stripped partly or entirely naked. Public nudity is another social fear that the drunk shamers exploit in these rituals. And the nonconsensual nudity opens up the wild side of erotics and bodily violation of drunk shaming: legally, much drunk shaming constitutes sexual assault, even if it is seldom seen as or prosecuted in this way. In conjunction with entirely or partially denuding the hapless drunk, things such as "ENTER" and "ENTER HERE" are often written on or near the buttocks of the person who is being defiled. So there is a strong sexual dimension to drunk shaming, whether or not sexual assault takes place. References to real or imagined sex acts work to intensify anxieties around sex, eroticism, homosexuality, and homoerotics while suggesting various forms of sexual violation.

There are some bizarre internal contradictions in all of this effort, on behalf of those engaging in a drunk shaming, to reinforce heterosexual norms. Take, for instance, the scenario that might have produced one widely circulated image of a drunk shaming: it is a photo of a naked young man who has passed out on a couch and is in the midst of a drunk shaming by a group of other men. He is stripped naked, written on, and covered in various fluids, including whipped cream. The inclusion of homoerotics in hazing rituals aimed at shoring up heteronormative norms has been noted by several critics writing about similar behaviors. Mark Simpson suggests, for instance, that homoerotics aim to emasculate the victims, and "the curious paradox of hazing is that while it may well regard 'fagginess' and 'softness' as undesirable, it actually makes the homoerotic central to membership of the group."[15] In drunk shamings, in many ways, social commonplaces and rules of propriety are suspended by those involved. Drunk shaming involves the use of writing (and other things) to at once break from the norms and reinforce them.

Anxieties are not the only things being worked out through drunk shamings. References to racial discrimination are also abundant in drunk shaming, with images of swastikas commonly drawn on faces and bodies. Some orchestrators of drunk shamings make their light-skinned victims wear blackface for the night. Just as straight might become gay, white becomes black as drunk shamers are not afraid to go to some of the most racist recesses of the cultural imaginary. In drunk shaming, swastikas exist right beside penises, black face, misogyny, and such things as silly moustaches and doodled drawings.

From the perspective of someone who studies and teaches about writing and rhetoric, it is typical to think of speakers addressing some audience in a particular situation or context. But in drunk shaming, the speakers (those doing the writing) ultimately become anonymous and practice a form of rhetorical ventriloquism, penning their crazy and offensive words and images on the body of their victim—and then, by nature of having to "wear" this new garment of disquieting expressions, the person who has been shamed becomes a kind of involuntary spokesperson for whatever has been written and drawn. Recall that in sign shaming, the signs often bear straightforward messages about some offense: "I am a bully" or "I am dishonest." In drunk shaming, the transposed author's only offense is passing out; what gets written creates an impermanent and often unfounded commentary about the person's character, supposed beliefs, and actions. The verbal cacophony of drunk shaming is solidified as the message worn by the person who has been shamed. The power of such body writing should not be underestimated as we live in a society where it is quite common for the messages we wear on our bodies (our printed T-shirts, for instance) to be associated with our personal beliefs.

Many of us spend much of our lives cultivating our most desirable versions of ourselves, in terms of how we look, what we wear, how we keep our hair, and what makeup we may or may not have on. A drunk-shaming episode quickly takes all of this away. In a drunk shaming, the ones doing the shaming temporarily wrest away the power of self-representation. Earlier in this chapter, I mentioned restroom graffiti as a somewhat similar vernacular writing practice. In drunk shaming, the person who is written on becomes a sort of textual equivalent of the heavily graffitied restroom stall. Like the restroom stall, all kinds of offensive and odd things are written, only there is no way of knowing who has written what. Drunk shaming, as the textual record indicates, is a similarly strong and anonymous form of defilement. Given the main activities associated with public restrooms, it is fitting that some of their walls would become homes to vulgar language. To take part in a drunk shaming and to peruse the images that result from them is to witness the (temporary) erasure and debasement of a person's richly cultivated identity. It may be painful to witness, even as the drunk shamings seem to largely be seen by the participants as humorous, hilarious pranks.

If drunk shamings were exceedingly rare and unusual, it would be easy to dismiss them as just another deviant, bizarre hiccup in modern life. But drunk shaming has become a widespread drinking ritual in particular social strata, and as a ritual the practice of carrying out a drunk shaming both makes and reflects some deep-seated understandings. Like many other cultural rituals (such as hazing and indoctrination rituals), orchestrating a drunk shaming means indulging in an urge to defile others in public. With the diminished inhibitions that come with alcohol consumption, such urges to write are more easily acted upon.

EMBODYING CONTRADICTIONS

Long before the advent of drunk shaming, erotics and literacy were imagined to come together on the body in Hieronymus Bosch's painting from 1500, *The Garden of Earthly Delights*. In case you are unfamiliar with Bosch's work, his paintings are highly symbolic, often include complicated narratives, and are densely packed with characters and other details. In *The Garden of Earthly Delights*, one of the tiny figures in the painting lies face down with his or her (it is hard to tell) naked buttocks exposed—and sheet music is written across them (fig. 3.2).

I mention this five-hundred-year-old painting not to steer the discussion into the realm of art history but because the painting is a vivid reminder that there has long been a novelty to or transgressive thrill in writing on someone's naked body. Also, the painting is a reminder to think about the people who are standing around reading what is written on the body. In Bosch's painting, one figure points to the written-on buttocks, a few others are singing, and a creature-figure appears to be singing the actual music that has been written on the person's rear end. I imagine that some version of this scene plays out in drunk-shaming incidents, with one or more people looking on, reading the newly written-on body. This painting is a reminder that drunk-shaming texts are created to be worn and read.

Recall that Audrie Pott was not only sexual assaulted and written on; images of her were circulated around her high school. Hundreds of drunk-shaming images can be seen online, reaching more readers than were present at the actual events. While these images have voyeuristic potential, photos of naked and seminaked victims of drunk shaming also represent just how damaging simple acts of writing can be.

When looked at in comparison with the other forms of writing-based punishments discussed thus far—schoolhouse punishments and sign shamings—drunk shaming is at once more impulsively bacchanalian,

Figure 3.2. Detail from Hieronymus Bosch's painting *The Garden of Earthly Delights* (1490–1500) at Museo del Prado in Madrid.

nonconsensual, and irregularly practiced. Discussing autonomy in the domain of medical law, Vibhav Mithal writes that "bodily integrity implies that the individual is the complete master of his own body and shall decide what is best for him even if in others' perceptions what he is doing is damaging to him."[16] This kind of respectful thinking is completely absent in drunk shaming. The images of people who have been drunk shamed contain a startlingly exuberant and profane use of writing on the body. The ways writing is used in drunk-shaming incidents reveals beliefs about writing as *both* redemptive and damning, hilarious and humiliating. In this way, drunk-shaming texts are not unlike the writing across the buttocks in the sixteenth-century painting by Bosch: the written-on buttocks make the civility of music possible, but only through the discord of the figure's nudity and prone position. Writing, in the ways it is used in drunk shaming, is turned to as a way to violate the individual by making the person advertise, via their very own skin, a cacophony of words, images, and ideas that almost no one would choose for themselves.

Drunk shaming encompasses a range of other contradictions: the bodies of those who pass out are decorated and given a lot of attention, and yet they are defaced; people are publically ridiculed via drunk shaming, and yet their uber-drunkenness is (at least partially) celebrated; and those who are targeted with drunk shaming are at once shunned and rewarded by being singled out. The limp body of the person in a drunk-shaming photograph is at once disciplined and disregarded in that he or she has been turned into what amounts to a living trash heap and a repository for the worst kinds of written words and drawn symbols. In all of these ways, writing is used to memorialize the confused and crazy energy of the party while making an expressive skin-garment of writing and images for the person to wear—if only for as long as it takes to find a good bar of soap and some hot water to wash it all off.

There is no one "significance" of drunk shaming. It is a way to use writing to preserve and memorialize the act of violating a helpless person. It is also a way that local forms of vernacular justice are meted out. *You passed out first at the party and you had your shoes on, so this is your sentence.* Drunk shamings produce ambiguity. And note that this kind of punishment, to the extent that it is punishment, is mutually agreed upon via the shared vernacular rules of the drunk-shaming ritual. But it is certainly not the case, as the name implies, that drunk shaming is simply a ritual aimed at shaming those who overdo it. To read drunk shaming in this way would be to suggest that this is one way for partygoers to promote moderation and sobriety. This is not entirely the case because drunk shaming is also the crowning of the party's biggest, most reckless, and committed drunk. With that said, it is still true that this is a drinking game that at least partially discourages rampant drunkenness and encourages moderation. There is at least one bottom line when it comes to drunk shaming: writing is used to produce shame and humiliation, and that happens through violating the personal space of the vulnerable person who is written on.

A recurring point in this book is my suggestion that people turn (at times) to writing in efforts to accomplish almost magical transformations of others. When writing is used as a disciplinary technology, in almost every situation I discuss, writing is thought by some to have the power to redeem, change, or reshape someone. While punishments involving writing might not logically and completely "work"—which is to say that writing "I will not chew gum in class" one thousand or one million times may not actually curb one's in-class gum chewing—writing gets used in these ways in part because it continues to be *seen* as having a potential to alter the writer. Writing, I think many of us believe and the ways it is used suggest, is thought to have its own alchemical force.

In the drunken din of parties where drunk shaming happens, these imaginings about what writing does and is capable of animate writers. When presented with an unconscious body at a party, most of us would like to think that we would see if the person is okay or call 911. We would be concerned. We would take care of the person. But participants in scenes where a drunk-shaming protocol is in place act very differently. They reach for their marking pens, performing rituals on and around the bodies of an overly intoxicated celebrant, adorning and writing on the torpid body. Said another way, they are motivated to write. Having watched several YouTube videos featuring live drunk shamings, I have the distinct impression that this kind of writing is thrilling for those doing the writing. The writing accomplishes something for the writers, then, and there is a belief that the writer, too, is transformed into a social deviant—if only temporarily in the semiprivate space of the party. This kind of writing, when seen in the light of day or online via video-sharing platforms, shows a lot of energy being put into elaborate attempts to remake (or rewrite) the bodies of those who are written on, turning them into living, breathing, yet only partially intelligible transcripts from the night before.

And to circle back around to my main point, a close look at drunk shaming reveals the widespread belief that writing is a viable way to violate another person. Writing is rarely seen in this light. Doctrine has it that writing is meant for the page, but nondoctrinal beliefs about writing are much more expansive, seeing it as fit for the body and a good way to make someone who has drunk too much wake up an entirely different person.

FOUR

FORCED TATTOOING

The typical tattoos that a pimp will use are dollar signs. They'll have a tattoo of a
money bag. They'll have a crown that stands for the whole pimping thing.

—Sgt. Ron Fisher, Los Angeles Police Department,
interview in *Branded: Sex Slavery in America*

Late in 2012, a Chicago man named Alex "Cowboy" Campbell was sentenced to life in prison for severely abusing several women and forcing
them into prostitution. In addition to raping and torturing the women,
court documents reveal that Campbell wrote all over them: specifically,
he had the women tattooed on their necks with matching horseshoe symbols, and at least two of the women were made to "receive tattoos on their
backs and wrists. Each woman received a tattoo covering 70 percent of her
back which depicted a scroll containing a manifesto drafted by Campbell
asserting that each woman 'live[s] for' Campbell 'till death'" (fig. 4.1). In
the present-day United States, tattoos have increasingly become a commonplace. Writing about the interconnectedness of tattoos and literacy, David E.
Kirkland refers to the tattoos one of his students had as a "human story of
literacy" that is "told in the workings of ink and flesh." One way that Alex
"Cowboy" Campbell deprived the women he exploited of controlling their
own "stories of literacy" was to forcibly tattoo them.[1]

The judge in the case sentenced Campbell to life in prison, stating in
court that the horrific nature of the crimes justified the punishment.
During sentencing, the judge said to the defendant: "I think the worst
thing you did to these girls, frankly, is branding [i.e., tattooing] them the
way you did. They can't get rid of those tattoos. . . . They have a life sentence, all of them. Every time they look in the mirror. . . . And it's gonna
hurt. Their life sentences compel a life sentence for you." So, in the words
of the judge, the life sentence was handed down because of the lasting pain

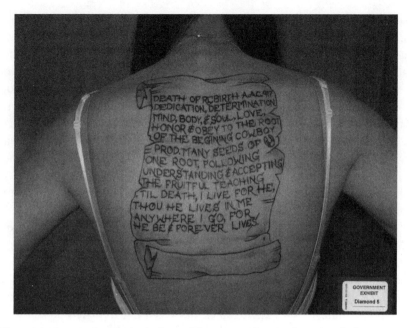

Figure 4.1. Photograph of the back of one of the women Alex "Cowboy" Campbell was convicted of abusing and forcibly tattooing in 2012. Photograph entered as evidence and reprinted in the *Chicago Tribune*, November 26, 2012.

inflicted by the tattoos. There is something troubling about this comment, as by foregrounding the importance of the tattoos, the judge minimizes the magnitude of Campbell's other crimes as a sex trafficker. With that said, the judge's shock and dismay at the forcibly applied tattoos is worth registering, as forcibly tattooing someone deprives that person of what Kirkland, referring to his tattooed student, calls "agency over inscription" or "how he is perceived in public spaces, and over how he could place himself and his meanings within a larger human context." Forced tattooing curtails how one's body is read and tries to limit what "one perceives as possible . . . through signs and symbols inscribed on paper or on flesh." In the US context, as I will discuss, such tattoos also refer back to a time when, as Shontavia Johnson and others have shown, "African and African-American slaves routinely had the initials or other identifying indicia of their slave masters permanently branded on their skin."[2]

By forcibly tattooing the women he exploited, Campbell was participating in a vernacular writing and marking practice used by human traffickers around the world. Whereas the ways that writing is used to punish and shame in classrooms, shame parades, and drunk-shaming incidents involve various kinds of ephemeral writing, forced tattooing asserts more permanent control via indelible writing on the body. Sex traffickers use brands and tattoos to process their victims into systems of human coercion and then to maintain their subordinate status as owned, dehumanized property. The degrading tattoos, which function much like trademarks, involve writing and other legible symbols that mark people as property much like livestock are marked by a brand or ear tag. As the late Jennifer Kempton, an outspoken advocate for the survivors of human trafficking, remarked, such tattoos are also used to produce a state of "psychological enslavement" in the minds of their victims. This form of writing tries to own, possess, and permanently define one as a sex worker through legible marks.[3]

In the United States, tattoos have enjoyed a surge in popularity in recent decades, with as many as 36 percent of Americans between the ages of eighteen and twenty-five sporting at least one tattoo.[4] The vast majority of those tattoos have been applied consensually, and the act of "getting a tattoo" is generally imbued with notions of freedom, self-determination, and cultural mystique. Mainstream tattoos represent everything from rebelliousness to personal expression to membership in a group, and this prevailing wisdom frames tattoos as symbols of personal expression. The examples I discuss in this chapter operate within a very different frame, as these tattoos have been imposed on people against their will and act as symbols of another person's method of control, linking the bearer of the tattoo with an abuser, activity, group, or some other undesirable message. In the examples I describe, the old adage about "the power of the written word" is intensified by words and phrases that are permanently inked onto the skin, literally defining the bearer of the tattoo as under the control of the person or group who has forcibly imposed the tattoo. In drunk shaming, writing is used to transform the victim for a short while, but forced tattooing is much more lasting.

The chapter begins with a brief history of forced tattooing then goes on to describe some excruciating stories of girls and women who have been forcibly tattooed within the system of human trafficking. I see this as the bleakest chapter in the book, but an important one in that it shows just how far people are willing to take the written word as a tool for establishing domination and control. I then go on to explain that human trafficking is not the only domain within which people are forcibly tattooed in contemporary life. While the bulk of the chapter focuses on forced tattoos in sex trafficking, I also discuss some contemporary instances of forcibly applied tattoos that have been used to enact various forms of extrajudicial justice and defamation. In these cases, citizens have used tattoos to set the record straight, so to speak, by tattooing a permanent word or phrase on their adversary. I end the chapter on what I hope is a high note by describing the work of Jennifer Kempton and others who have worked to fund cover-ups of forcibly applied tattoos in efforts to aid the victims and survivors of sex trafficking.

In some ways, the examples in this chapter are a far cry from scenes of schoolchildren being made to write "I will not chew gum in class" or people being made to hold handwritten signs on street corners. But forced tattooing is similar to writing lines in a classroom in that writing remains seen as alchemical stuff that can transform and control someone, and forced tattooing is like sign shaming and drunk shaming in relying on the dynamics of transposed authorship to make the bearer of the tattoo a sort of spokesperson for the message that someone else has written. In forced tattooing, legible tattoos are used to try to control and transform the tattooed person through interaction with an audience who sees and reads the tattoo. I also argue that by being made to permanently "wear" a legible marker—large or small—the victims of forced tattooing become not only bearers of the messages inked into their flesh but unwilling advertisements for, of all things, claims to literacy on behalf of their oppressors.

SOME HISTORY

To understand contemporary forced tattooing in the United States, it is worth considering some distant historical contexts in which other forced tattoos have been used to mark, label, and control such people as slaves, criminals, and prisoners. What follows is by no means intended as a comprehensive history of forced tattooing but more of a brief glimpse into the historical record to help understand the meanings and motivations behind contemporary uses of forcibly applied written tattoos.

In an array of ancient and modern cultures, criminals and slaves were routinely forcibly tattooed and branded. One of the most iconic and legible examples of tattooing criminals took place in Japan from the seventeenth through the nineteenth centuries. During this period, iconic forehead tattoos (called *irezumi kei*, or the "tattoo penalty") were inked onto convicted criminals, with each tattoo—symbolic dots, lines, and other marks—representing different crimes. These tattoos worked to visibly label someone, attaching the person to a crime, and the forehead was used to make the label obvious to others.[5]

Forced tattooing also took place much earlier in the Mediterranean region and Middle East. As David Brion Davis writes: "Permanent branding or tattooing was . . . common in Egypt, the Neo-Babylonian Empire, Roman Sicily, and even fifteenth-century Tuscany. From the earliest times such skin markings became indelible signs of a servile status, and suggested a deformity of character which deserved contempt." Such forcibly applied tattoos not only recorded previous behaviors but were used to affect status and perceptions of character. As Adrienne Mayor writes, prisoners of war and slaves were tattooed in Greece and Egypt as early as 500 BC, and these "tattoos were not carefully or artistically applied. Ink was poured into crude letters carved into the flesh." The crude nature of the tattoos degraded and defiled slaves and prisoners through the stigma of the marks. Deborah Kamen confirms this view, writing that "chattel slaves [in ancient Athens] were defined at least in part by the fact that, unlike free people, they had to answer for their wrongdoings with their bodies."[6]

Writing about the context of US slavery, where brands and tattoos were also used on enslaved people, Shontavia Johnson describes how tattoos were applied to manage humans as financial property: "Prior to the passage of state and federal trademark law, slave owners used trademarks as a way to distinguish their human property from the property of other slave masters." Individual slaveholders applied trademark tattoos, and nations were known to tattoo all slaves in a country with the national mark. Slaves were tattooed with trademarks to assert and maintain economic ownership over them, assuring that the wealth that came from their labor was maintained and controlled.[7]

In the past century, perhaps the most recognizable and iconic use of forced tattooing was at the Auschwitz concentration camp complex, where an estimated four hundred thousand prisoners were tattooed with identifying letters, numbers, and icons. Most prisoners were tattooed on the forearm, and after the war, the tattoos came to be seen as both a symbol of the dehumanizing Nazi regime and the perseverance of survivors. While the primary logic behind these concentration camp tattoos was to keep track of prisoners, the tattoos simultaneously worked to demean and torture, as many of the numbers were applied with a single spiked stamp. As Edwin Black has shown in his 2008 book *IBM and the Holocaust*, the serial-number system the Nazis used in the tattoos was derived from the five-digit Hollerith organizational numbers developed by IBM. So the tattoos were part of a larger techno-governmental system used to track and manage Jews, prisoners of war, and other people deemed dissident.[8]

It is important to look back at these examples of forced tattooing and branding from such disparate cultural and historical contexts for several reasons. The first is to emphasize that the use of forced tattooing in the contemporary world is neither new nor innovative. Instead, it derives from over a millennia of previous instances in which forced tattoos have been used. Second, there is a commonality among all of these historical examples in that the tattoos tend to work simultaneously to mark the tattooed individual as a slave, criminal, or prisoner *and* to subordinate the social status of the tattooed person via the marks. In addition, forced tattoos have been used to maintain such things as economic control and order. Marks on the forehead, which I will return to toward the end of the chapter, have been used to speak to specific crimes while signaling that one has been made to submit to the state. Similarly, marks on the arm like those used at Auschwitz signal that one is being managed like a branded animal.[9]

And yet, there is a key difference between these historical instances of forced tattooing and the ones I am about to describe: in all of the historical cases I have discussed, the forced tattoos were state sponsored in one way or another. All of the slaves, criminals, and prisoners I have described were tattooed either by the state itself; by an arm of the state, such as the SS at Auschwitz; or via acts that were state sponsored, as was the case when slaveholders in the United States branded and tattooed trademarks on the enslaved peoples they controlled. In the contemporary examples I discuss, none of the tattooing is state sponsored or even legal. Nonetheless, these contemporary tattooing practices draw directly from their historical, state-sponsored precedents in terms of how the tattoos work via marking, degrading, regulating, and controlling with legible writing and other marks on the body.

FORCED TATTOOS IN SEX TRAFFICKING

Human trafficking is typically described as consisting of sex trafficking and labor trafficking (though both involve forced labor, just of different kinds), and the victims of sex trafficking are frequently tattooed against their will. The tattoos include such things as the names of sex traffickers and other symbols that mark and establish ownership over their victims. These marks function as pseudo trademarks, with current US trademark law defining trademarks as "any word, name, symbol, or device . . . [used] to identify and distinguish [the trademark owner's] goods, including a unique product, from those manufactured or sold by others and to indicate the source of the goods, even if that source is unknown." As pseudotrademarks, the tattoos are part of a process of transforming a person into property and maintaining that person as an ongoing source of revenue through sex work. Sex trafficking has been referred to by many, including the State Department, as "modern slavery," and I do not pretend to do justice, here, to all that is entailed in the wide range of very serious human rights violations involved in sex trafficking. Instead, this chapter focuses on the use of writing, in the form of forced tattoos, in what the FBI refers to as the "commercial sex industry."[10]

A focus on the role of tattoos in sex trafficking risks minimizing the many other atrocities that are integral to this industry. To avoid this, let me just say that the central problem in sex trafficking is certainly not the tattoos. However, it is worth focusing on the tattoos in sex trafficking because (1) they are one way that sex traffickers maintain their power, and (2) the tattoos are connected to other forms of writing as punishment. These forcibly applied tattoos are not an aberration taking place only on the shady margins of society. Instead, the logic behind their use bears similarity to the logic behind much more sanctified uses of writing as a disciplinary technology in schools, courtrooms, and parties. The dominion that sex traffickers attempt to impose (in part) via forcibly applied tattoos is related in some rather frightening ways to other examples in this book.

There is no way of knowing how many victims of sex trafficking are forcibly tattooed, but many sources indicate that the practice is common and has become increasingly reported on and documented in recent years. I have found dozens of documented examples of this kind of tattooing from around the globe, with descriptions of such tattoos appearing consistently in US court records. The practice of forcibly tattooing girls and women who are victims of sex trafficking is widespread, with many police and social service organizations being aware of it. Studies estimate numbers of sex-trafficking cases worldwide to be in the millions annually.[11]

The tattoos sex traffickers use follow certain patterns and logics. The tattoos are often names and symbols that mark the girls and women, much like brands are used to mark ownership over cattle and other animals. At the most basic level, these legible, symbolic tattoos are deployed to do the same kinds of things as the other forms of writing-based punishments discussed in this book: the tattoos aim to transform victims, and by nature of being indelible marks on the flesh, this kind of writing aims to make the transformation permanent. In sex trafficking, tattoos are a way to induct victims into the position of being subject to human bondage. These forced tattoos are some of the most deviant and cruel uses of writing as punishment, and this particular kind of writing on the body shows the extent to which literate acts can be integral to systems of degradation and regulation.

Having examined these tattoos, I see them as having three main functions: they demean, brand, and attempt to reflect certain forms of literacy (on behalf of the traffickers).

Tattooing to Demean

I began this chapter with the case of Alex "Cowboy" Campbell, the Chicago man who, in 2012, was convicted of abusing several women, forcing them into prostitution, and requiring at least two of the women to have their backs tattooed with large scrolls of his design (see fig. 4.1). The massive back tattoos convey many messages at once—in terms of what they literally say but also via their placement, size, and overall style.

The actual text of the tattoos is bizarre and rewards close reading. It begins with a self-aggrandizing reference to Campbell's birthdate (9/17) and then goes on to celebrate Campbell as a teacher and quasi-religious figure endowed with eternal life. Without correcting any of the nonstandard spelling, grammar, or phrasings, the full tattoo reads: "Death of rebirth A.A.C. 917 dedication, determination, mind, body, & soul. Love, honor & obey to the root of the begining Cowboy Prod. many seeds of one root, following understanding & accepting the fruitful teaching til death, I live for he, thou he lives in me, anywhere I go, for he be & forever lives." Reading the tattoo for the first time, the rambling text seems part incantation, part poem, and part declaration. In several ways, "Cowboy" has made himself the main character in this quasi-religious "scroll," and the women are the vehicle for him to become published. Campbell is not depicted as a criminal abuser in the tattoo but as both a teacher ("accepting the fruitful teaching til death") and supreme being ("I live for he, thou he lives in me, anywhere I go, for he be & forever lives"), who has the ability to perpetually follow and be part of the women via the tattoo. The handwritten, quasi-calligraphic aesthetics of the text lends it the style of a decree written on parchment, trying to promote Campbell as someone endowed with traditional forms of sanctioned authority.

In addition to the literal meanings of the tattoo, its placement and size tries to assert his dominance. Court documents from the case reveal that Campbell insisted on new names for the women he controlled (they were all recent immigrants to the United States), even referring to one of the women by the name he imposed on her ("Trinity") during court proceedings. In the tattoos and in his use of new names, Campbell used language to establish and maintain his power. By taking the names of his victims away from them and covering the women with large tattooed writing of his own design, Campbell worked hard to establish a symbolic system that demeaned and possessed the women he abused and controlled.

While the particular tattoos Campbell used are unique, his techniques are not unusual. In a widely reported 2014 case of sex trafficking in Poland, a group of women who were compelled to work in a brothel were elaborately tattooed with phrases and such things as the names of their captors. Within the context of the Polish brothel where the women were forced to work, the tattoos were framed as "rewards" for subservience and hard work. The names of sex traffickers were written in giant tattoos across the bodies of the women; other tattoos said such things as (translated into English) "I love my Lord and Master, property of Leszek" and "faithful bitch of Leszek."[12] This type of demeaning and controlling tattooing is not unusual within the realm of sex trafficking, and some of the more calligraphic tattoos seem to be efforts to eroticize the women with elegant writing. These tattoos reveal how written language is integral to a larger system of exploitation that relies on and tries to sustain the transformation of the person being tattooed.

These kinds of forcibly applied tattoos not only make overt claims that the women who bear the tattoos are property, but the tattoos carry an implied argument that the women are not in control of their own bodies and the messages they convey. This is another way that the tattoos achieve a base level of degradation. In the much more common arena of voluntary tattooing, those of us who have tattoos probably chose both the tattoos we got and where they were placed on our bodies. In a contemporary US context, this is because most tattoos are generally thought to epitomize free expression. But in the case of a tattoo that has been forcibly applied, such choices are taken away from the victim. This gives the tattoos an additional and implicit message: the bearer of the forced tattoo has been deprived of her ability and right to express herself via her own body. The very act of tattooing a message on the body of another person against her will works to make that person appear (symbolically) lowly, demeaned, and less than human—when being human is defined as having basic levels of self-determination and control. Writing, in the form of these forced tattoos, is a tool that helps these deplorable accomplishments get realized, at least in part, in the world of sex trafficking.

Tattooing to Brand
There was a telling moment in the sentencing hearing for Alex "Cowboy" Campbell when the judge referred to the tattoos as brands. The judge told

Campbell: "I think the worst thing you did to these girls, frankly, is branding them the way you did." The court documents do not mention that Campbell literally branded the women with hot irons; instead the judge in the case was referring to Campbell's use of tattoos as if they were brands. The documentary *Branded: Sex Slavery in America*, also refers to such tattoos as brands. Brands are not tattoos, but the two are referred to interchangeably with some frequency in the context of sex trafficking. This slippage makes sense, as the tattoos sex traffickers use function a lot like the brands that are used to mark some livestock: the tattoos are used to control humans as if they were inventory.

To see how this works, recall that not only did Campbell forcibly apply the large back tattoos. He also imposed small horseshoe tattoos (his "Cowboy" brand) on the women he controlled. Such legible symbols function much like brands, marking victims with symbols that refer back to a so-called owner. As Sgt. Ron Fisher of the Los Angeles Police Department remarks in the documentary *Branded*, "the typical tattoos that a pimp will use are dollar signs. They'll have a tattoo of a money bag. They'll have a crown that stands for the whole pimping thing." In 2011, San Diego public radio station KPBS reported on the sexual exploitation of a teenager referred to as Lisa (a pseudonym). Lisa, a minor, was drugged, raped, and received a brand-like tattoo on the inside of her bottom lip noting the name, Richey, of her victimizer. In 2013, several news agencies reported on a similar story of a Miami teenage girl who was forced to have the nickname of the man who exploited her tattooed across her eyelids and on her upper chest. The girl was thirteen years old. In a recent case in Texas, a young woman "had the word 'Stash' [the nickname of her trafficker] surrounded by stars and a dollar sign tattooed on her right thigh." In a case in California in 2009, a woman was tattooed with the word "Payroll," the brand of the man who trafficked her. In another case in California in May of 2015, two underage girls were forced into prostitution and the men who controlled them "forced the 15-year-old to tattoo their nicknames on her shoulders." There are even cases of barcodes being forcibly tattooed on victims. There is an economic, brand-like dimension to all of these tattoos, with one goal being to assure that the earnings of trafficked women come back to the "owner" of the brand.[13]

Early on in this chapter, I mentioned that the tattoos people received at Auschwitz in the 1940s originated from five-digit IBM Hollerith numbers, and a principle purpose of the Auschwitz tattoos was to sort, track, and organize an imprisoned workforce. Within the domain of sex trafficking, tattoos also track and manage people in a system of commerce. In no case is this economic purpose of these tattoos more evident than in a human trafficking ring that was broken up in Spain in 2012. A headline in the *Daily Mail* reads: "Pimps Tattooed BAR CODE on Wrist of Woman Imprisoned, Whipped and Forced to Work as a Prostitute."[14] In this case, which was widely reported on by multiple news outlets, a group of women were controlled and exploited, with some of them (including at least one teenager) being forced to receive wrist tattoos that included both a bar code and an amount of money that was reputedly owed as a debt to the captors. The bar code, or UPC symbol, is the inventory-managing brand of our time, and its use in these instances of human trafficking works to reduce humans to the status of revenue-generating commodities that are bought and sold.

Tattooed brands shore up, assert, and maintain possession in sex trafficking, as many of these tattoos are much simpler and more scannable than the large back tattoos that Campbell forced upon the women he exploited. My survey of court records and news reports reveals many such tattoos.

Jennifer Kempton, whose work I discuss in more detail at the end of this chapter, was an outspoken advocate for the survivors of sex trafficking. In interviews with Kempton and in her public lectures, she described how she was inducted into sex trafficking then tattooed by a man who "sold" her to another man who also tattooed her. One of Kempton's tattoos was overt about her status: it read "Property of Salem." "It didn't matter what I'd say or do," Kempton remarked in a 2014 interview in the *Guardian*. "The tattoo sent a message to everyone that I was owned and was not my own person." At another point in the same interview, Kempton remarked: "I was branded like cattle." These tattoo brands dehumanize, control, establish ownership, and by being indelible, create what Kempton was keen to describe as a particular kind of psychic and emotional trauma.[15]

While some might be tempted to think of a symbolic tattoo as easy to cover up or as "only writing," the tattoos I have described attempt to establish and maintain genuinely subhuman positions for the bearers of these marks. Now, I am not saying that the tattoos are always successful in accomplishing all that they set out to do, and I would not suggest that these tattoos do all the work, on their own, of demeaning and dehumanizing the victims of sex trafficking. But tattoo-brands are clearly integral to the complex, destructive systems of sex trafficking. A wide array of horrifying methods are used to control the victims of sex trafficking, with tattoos being one part of the system of exploitation. What these forcibly applied tattoos represent is clear: the women who are forced to bear these tattooed marks are, in the words of Jennifer Kempton, "branded like cattle" for the gain of others.

Forced Tattooing and Literacy

It is worth reasking the simple question that I have posed several times in this book: What significance is there in the fact that it is writing, of all things, that sex traffickers use as a tool for punishment and control? Why use writing?

While not all of the tattoos used by sex traffickers involve written words—there are the horseshoe symbols, the dollar signs, the crowns, and the barcodes that I mentioned—many of the tattoos do involve some sort of writing. The names of sex traffickers are most common, but other phrases and sentences are also used. Recall that one of Kempton's tattoos read "Property of Salem," and this kind of phrasing is not uncommon. In these tattoos, writing (of all things) is used to dehumanize and track victims. Written names, phrases, and entire paragraphs are used to do some of the work, if we can call it that, of the sex trafficker. Writing, when forcibly applied as a tattoo, helps sex traffickers create a set of marked bodies that benefit them.

Because writing appears as a feature of these tattoos, they take on an added level of meaning as examples of literacy in the way that the tattoos represent (or attempt to represent) the sex traffickers, who employ the tattoos as literate people and who use writing as part of their work. The long scroll-like tattoo that Alex "Cowboy" Campbell painfully foisted on his victims is a far cry from a literary masterpiece, but it is an attempt to use a literary form (the poem) to dominate. With writing, Campbell attempted to claim the status of someone who can proclaim, attest, avow, and own via the sanctioned mechanisms of writing. Textual tattoos of all kinds help sex traffickers (in part) perpetrate their crimes, and the traffickers tap into (or attempt to tap into) aspects of the larger cultural cachet of the written word. Now, you might not think that these tattoos make the people who impose them on their victims look comparable to other published authors, but I think it is worth thinking about how these tattoos leverage at least some of the value and authority that other forms of writing can have in very different contexts.

I am not saying that the forced tattoos sex traffickers inflict on their victims successfully represent these criminals as sophisticated writers, but forced tattooing is a way that sex traffickers exploit some of the cachet of written language. This explains another part of why writing, of all things, is integral to sex trafficking. Note that writing is generally seen as having an element of power and prestige associated with it; writing is linked to such things as education, class ascendency, and civility. The tattoos used at Auschwitz were not thoughtless and unsophisticated; they were part of a complex system of empirical dominance. Similarly, forced textual tattoos are part of a system of textual dominance that sex traffickers exploit to maintain their networks of control.

TATTOOS AND EXTRAJUDICIAL JUSTICE

In our time, tattoos applied within the horrific world of sex trafficking are by far the most prevalent instances of forced tattooing. However, there are other current examples of tattoos being forcibly applied in other contexts and for other reasons. As I have discussed, in the domain of sex trafficking, tattoos are largely used to demean, control, and manage. In other contexts, tattoos are used to achieve what I describe as extrajudicial justice—or justice accomplished by vigilantes working outside of the court system. In these examples, individuals use forced tattooing to respond to perceived forms of injustice, using tattoos as tools of lasting punishment. These tattooers tap into long histories of nations tattooing convicted criminals—only here the tattooers have taken the law into their own hands.

A vivid example of this is a 2006 case in Indiana: state prison inmate Anthony Ray Stockelman had the words "Katie's Revenge" tattooed in large letters across his forehead by fellow inmates. Media widely reported the attack on Stockelman when a photo of Stockelman's freshly tattooed face was leaked to the press.[16] To understand how this tattoo can be seen as an attempt to accomplish extrajudicial justice, you need to know that Stockelman was incarcerated for molesting and murdering a young girl named Katie. The crude tattoo appears to have been intended to serve as additional, "jailhouse punishment" for the crime. The forehead tattoo is not unlike the once popular branding of criminals that was ratified by the 1547 Statute of Vagabonds in Britain. Just as many types of criminals were forced to bear brands that made their criminal past publically apparent to all, Stockelman was compelled to bear a lasting reference to his crime and victim.

A similar incident took place four years later in 2010. News agencies reported that Australian teenager Steven Jiminez had been tattooed with the word "Dog" across his forehead in large letters. The tattoo was applied by another man, Jason Tattersall, who claimed that Jiminez had slept with Tattersall's girlfriend while Tattersall was in prison. This kind of writing on the body is reminiscent of drunk shaming but with higher stakes. As in the previous example, the forehead tattoo was applied in response to a (perceived) wrongdoing. In this case, the "Dog" tattoo aimed to demean Jiminez, as well as permanently mark him with a reference to his "low," doglike character. In another example from Singapore in 2007, a man who suspected his wife of infidelity conspired with a tattoo artist to forcibly tattoo her breast, abdomen, and forearms. The tattoos were meant to "punish" her for what the man saw as her offenses. In an earlier case from California in the 1990s, two gang members kidnapped a teenage member of a rival gang, beat and tortured him, wrote "gang related graffiti on his body," and forcibly tattooed him. The tattoos were a form of gang-related retaliation, thus justified within the culture of gang rivalry. In yet another example, a Mayfair, Pennsylvania, man was forcibly tattooed with "a dozen racist and sexually explicit tattoos" after being accused of injuring a cat. Yes, a cat.[17]

Note just how differently these forced tattoos work when compared to the use of tattoos within the context of sex trafficking. In these cases, the tattoos were applied to permanently associate a person with some kind of (real or imagined) wrongdoing. The tattoos are often placed in plain view (this is why the forehead is commonly used) and as such work to publically shame and humiliate those who are tattooed. In all instances of forced tattooing, an indelible message is written upon a person who must bear the significance of the tattoo indefinitely, but here the tattoo is used as a vernacular form of public punishment for misdeeds. Just as many types of criminals were once tattooed by various nations, so are these individuals tattooed extrajudicially by rogue vigilantes and groups. In this kind of forced tattooing, though, what is deemed "a crime" or unjust is entirely determined by the person doing the tattooing.

SURVIVOR'S INK

In Stieg Larsson's novel, *The Girl with the Dragon Tattoo*, Lisbeth, the protagonist, is sexually assaulted by someone she is supposed to trust: her legal guardian. To get her revenge on him, Lisbeth forcibly tattoos the man with the words "I am a rapist and a sadistic pig" then threatens to carve the words into his forehead if he gets the tattoo removed. This aggressive reversal of power has a triumphant tone in the novel and films, as Lisbeth's act of revenge with the forcibly applied tattoo seems ingenious, innovative, and justified.

While the tattoos and other wrongs perpetrated by sex traffickers in real life are not avenged in the same way as they are in *The Girl with the Dragon Tattoo*, there is some justice being done to right these wrongs. Activist groups are challenging the permanent forms of control and exploitation that forced tattoos attempt to assert. For some who survive sex trafficking and go on to build new lives, repairing the damage that was done to them can involve removing or remaking their tattoos. Jennifer Kempton, who

I have mentioned several times already, was one example of a survivor working to reverse the power asserted by sex traffickers via compulsory tattoos. In 2014, Kempton established a project called Survivor's Ink (www. survivorsink.org) to help other survivors of sex trafficking move on with their lives no matter the scars they bear, including tattoos. The nonprofit group Kempton started, which is based in Ohio, provides grants for tattooed survivors of sex trafficking to have the tattoos they were subjected to removed or written over with new content. Kempton, who died in 2017, described the removal or covering up of existing, forcibly applied tattoos as nothing short of liberation from the symbolic system of bondage. Gang insignias are made into flowers, and "property of" tattoos are covered over with new messages.

In an article published in 2014 in the *Guardian*, a survivor who was able to remake and cover over her old tattoos, thanks to Survivor's Ink, is quoted as saying: "Every time I looked at that tattoo it took me back there to a lot of bad memories. I was trying to brush it off like it never happened and it never mattered—but it did, it did matter, so I felt very grateful for the opportunity to get the ownership of my body back. Getting the new tattoo has been a lot of how I've been able to recover and work on the scars inside."[18] Like most writing, the forcibly applied textual tattoos in situations of sex trafficking are not as permanent as the people perpetrating the tattoos would like them to be, and Kempton's group works to reshape the texts into new kinds of meaning overlaid on the old.

Other nonprofit organizations in the United States also focus on removing and remaking tattoos that were forced upon the victims of sex trafficking. One such group is Ink180, which removes and remakes gang-related tattoos as well as those suffered by the victims of sex trafficking. Chris Baker, the founder of Ink180, is informed by a similar philosophy and mission as Jennifer Kempton. He works to "transform the painful reminders of the destructive situations into beautiful art by covering the tattoos left from a former life in a gang or enslaved by human trafficking." Tattoos used in human trafficking are far from being "mere writing"—they are a powerful legacy that some survivors have the chance to deal with and remove. In Milwaukee, people bearing the marks of sex trafficking can go to Kate Malone at Atomic Tattoos to have their forcibly applied tattoos removed.[19]

While these efforts to help tattooed survivors purge their skin of the written records of sex trafficking operate on a rather small scale, some states in the United States have begun to offer financial support for tattoo removal. In 2012, the state of California passed Assembly Bill No. 1956, which expanded the reach of the already existing California Voluntary Tattoo Removal Program. The program formerly only served former gang members, allowing people affiliated with the Department of Corrections and Rehabilitation and between the ages of fourteen and twenty-four to have unwanted tattoos removed. The expansion of the California Voluntary Tattoo Removal Program in 2012 meant that those "who were tattooed for identification in trafficking or prostitution" could also be helped. The Crime Victims Compensation Act in Illinois provides similar resources for victims, covering "costs associated with trafficking tattoo removal by a person authorized or licensed to perform the specific removal procedure." In New Hampshire, a similar law ("Relative to Trafficking in Persons") was passed in 2014, covering up to $25,000 in medical care for victims—including tattoo removal.

I end this chapter on forced tattooing with this relative high note because, while writing can be used in many ways to control, punish, and dominate others, these forces that writing helps exert can also be deflected, redirected, and reversed. Even a forcibly applied written tattoo is, after all, only writing. For survivors of sex trafficking who are fortunate enough to have the forcibly applied tattoos on their bodies removed, the act of tattoo removal or covering up is an important symbolic act. These tattoo removal efforts show both the power of the tattoos and the ways that their presence can be quickly undermined and diminished.

In the next and final chapter, I return to the courts to discuss yet another way that writing is used to control and punish.

FIVE

WRITING, SELF-REFLECTION, AND JUSTICE

This paper required that [my assailant] read an article on Emerging Adulthood, and then write a minimum of 5–7 pages that reflected on the developmental tasks of this phase of his life. The paper asked for him to evaluate where he was in adulthood, what areas of adulthood had he ignored, and where did he want to go from there.

—Sarah Gilchriese, "Organizational Discourse and Discursive Closure on College Sex Assault"

Sarah Gilchriese, the author of the epigraph to this chapter, was raped by a fellow student at the University of Colorado at Boulder—and for part of his punishment, Gilchriese's assailant was made to write a paper. Gilchriese sued the University of Colorado at Boulder for damages, the university settled the case, and Gilchriese went on to write her undergraduate thesis about the experience. Administrators at the University of Colorado are not alone in choosing to punish a student rapist with writing. In 2012, a sexual assault at UC Berkley got a similar response, with the rapist being made to "complete a reflective writing assignment." At Wheaton College in Illinois, five college football players faced felony charges after allegedly abducting a fellow teammate, stripping him half-naked, and attempting to sodomize him. College administrators responded by requiring the assailants to do community service work and write eight-page reflective essays. The 2012 documentary film on the topic of campus rape, *The Hunting Ground*, captures how these writing-based slaps on the wrist are all too common on college campuses, where expository writing seems to be seen as a cure-all. On many campuses, including the one where I teach, when students violate underage drinking rules, they may have to write a "reflective essay." When reflective writing is used to punish a crime as serious as rape, the rehabilitative capacities of writing are inflated while the offense is trivialized.[1]

These writing-based punishments are not only used on college campuses. The US court system widely applies similar punishments. The following headlines, taken from recent news articles, tell a story about the use of writing in criminal sentencing in courts of law: "Man Convicted in Noose Attack Ordered to Write Essay on Lychings," "Drug Dealer Is Ordered to Write 5,000 Word Essay," "Write a Book Report, Avoid Jail: Judge Orders Man Freed If He Commits to Literature," "Cops Make Students Riding on Footboard Write Imposition," "Woman Sentenced to Write Apology Letter to City," "Man Made to Write Lines for Stealing Nude Portrait," "Federal Judge Requires Richmond Robbery Defendant to Submit Book Reports While Free on Bond."[2]

Hate crimes. Weapons charges. Drug-dealing. Theft. Writing has been used as punishment for these crimes and more.

In this final chapter, I explore legal cases in which judges have required defendants to write letters of apology, essays, and book reports. I return to a question that has informed much of this book: What beliefs about writing are made visible by examining how it is used as punishment? The first and easiest way to answer this question is to show, in the examples that follow, that writing is thought to be capable of creating deep, lasting kinds of reform in writers. But there is much more to the adoption of writing-based punishments by the judges who use them. Writing-based punishments can create the impression that judges care little about certain crimes, while framing the criminals who commit them as needing only minimal diversion to get back on the straight and narrow. In addition, when judges "assign" reading and writing in their courts, they reinforce a nostalgic idea that conventional forms of writing, once foundational to an education system, create law-abiding citizens. The writing-based legal sentences I describe construe the crimes they respond to as the result of deficits in knowledge and education—as opposed to large-scale and complex societal factors. If only the offender would have *known more*, or *learned more in school*, then his or her crime would never have been committed. And by relation, since writing-based legal sentences can only be imposed on the literate, those who cannot read and write are framed as existing outside the pale of this particular kind of edification. It might be easy to dismiss the writing-based legal sentences I describe in this chapter as mere busy work assigned to kill time. But I see them as indicators of deep-seated beliefs in writing, even when it is involuntarily initiated, as being able to redeem and restore the moral character of writers, and these sentences use mandated forms of writing to support the presumption that crime is the fault of bad schools, poor teachers, and inadequate amounts of writing in the first place.

In order to explain these arguments, I begin with an overview of some of the developments in legal philosophy that have made these writing-based legal sentences recently appealing to some judges. While writing-based punishments have been meted out by judges in the United States since at the least the 1930s, an uptick of such sentences in recent years is the result of increasing investment in the legal philosophy known as *restorative justice*. After providing a brief overview of the restorative justice model, I delve into some bizarre recent court cases in which sitting judges have incorporated apology letters, essays, and book reports into legal sentences. When these judges use writing for the purposes of justice, they tap into the many varied ways that writing is used as punishment culture-wide. In particular, these cases indicate a belief in writing as having quasi-mystical punitive and redemptive powers that can be used to curb criminality.

FROM RETRIBUTIVE TO RESTORATIVE JUSTICE, A QUICK OVERVIEW

Systems of punishment are always evolving. How and why, in the Western legal tradition, did gory scenes of public punishment (such as drawing and quartering) fall out of favor and get replaced with approaches such as incarceration and probation? In *Discipline and Punish*, Michel Foucault describes the many mechanisms that led to what he calls the "disappearance of torture as a public spectacle."[3] For Foucault, the move away from torturing the bodies of criminals in public is not as benevolent as it might seem; the change to seemingly cleaner, "nicer" punishments masked an insidious move toward working on the mind and soul of the condemned.

Up until about fifty years ago, operative theories of justice in the United States were largely retributive in nature and informed by philosophers such as Immanuel Kant and Jeremy Bentham. Kant argued that severe and fair punishment was justified ("whoever has committed a murder must die") as long as the punishment was meted out fairly: after one is "found guilty and punishable," one can be justly punished. Jeremy Bentham similarly wrote that there was value in punishment as a deterrent: restraint, for Bentham, comes about because "a man [may] not . . . be able to do the act, whatever it be, which by the apprehension of the punishment he is deterred from doing." Foucault wrote quite a bit about Bentham as an architect (literally and figuratively) of modern retributive justice that has the power to efficiently control and punish criminals without leaving marks on their bodies. In H. L. A. Hart's classic work on crime and punishment from 1968, *Punishment and Responsibility*, Hart frames traditional punishment as aimed at the "protection of society from dangerous criminals, rehabilitation, and (most of all) deterrence." In the most basic sense, the retributive model makes an example of the criminal.[4]

This focus on deterrence in the retributive justice model has been questioned by a new paradigm of legal philosophy known as restorative justice. The essence of restorative justice is captured by Van Ness and Strong in their 2014 book *Restoring Justice*. This way of thinking insists that the justice system can do more than punish: it can and should recognize victim's needs and engage convicted criminals in repairing the damage they have caused. In the restorative justice paradigm, breaking the law means being held accountable to and by those who have been injured, with the justice system facilitating a process of reconciliation and restitution. In the UK, legal sentences that are informed by this restorative justice philosophy are referred to as *direct practical reparation* and include such things as making restitution and crafting verbal and written apologies to victim(s). Criminals are not just "made examples of" but instead are expected to do the work needed to repair the damages they have brought about. Writing, in the form of apology letters, is frequently taken up to do this repair work. Frank D. Hill writes that "restorative practice often involves apology or other formal acknowledgements of the harm one has caused" and goes on to say that "acknowledging responsibility under a restorative model plays out very differently than in the traditional justice system: restorative justice involves the offender in the crafting of what will be done to 'put things right.'"[5]

Another factor informing the recent popularity of writing-based legal sentences is that it has become fashionable for some judges in the United States and UK to hand out creative and unusual legal sentences. These sentences garner attention for the judges in the media while challenging traditional sentencing. One judge in Ohio is particularly well-known for these kinds of unique, attention-getting sentences: Judge Michael Cicconetti has required such things as long walks for failing to pay a cab fare, sleeping out in the woods for abandoning kittens, and wearing a chicken suit in public for soliciting prostitutes. Most writing-based sentences are informed to a greater or lesser degree by the appealing nature of creative sentencing and the legal philosophy of restorative justice.[6]

LETTERS OF APOLOGY AS WINDOWS TO THE SOUL

In 2013, a Pennsylvania Supreme Court justice, Joan Orie Melvin, was convicted of taking part in an elaborate campaign corruption scheme and sentenced to house arrest, fined $55,000, and disbarred. The influence of restorative justice informed two additional parts of her sentence: she was made to work in a soup kitchen and forced to write several letters of apology. Her sentence stipulated that the letters be addressed to "(1) all sitting judges and justices in Pennsylvania, and (2) all former members of her judicial staff and the staff of her sister, former state senator Jane Orie." (The two sisters had taken part in the crimes together.) In an attempt to humiliate and humble the former justice, the sentencing judge stipulated that the letters be sent along with copies of a photograph of Melvin taken "by the court photographer while she was wearing handcuffs."[7]

Legal sentences that include letters of apology have become increasingly common in the United States, and such cases routinely capture the attention of journalists and legal scholars alike. To show just how common these kinds of writing-based sentences are, here is a snapshot of such cases reported in the media during *a two-week period* in January 2015: In Nashua, New Hampshire, a man was convicted of domestic violence and required to write a letter of apology as part of his sentence. In Canyon City, Colorado, a man pleaded guilty to burglary and was made to write letters of apology to the people he had stolen from. A woman in Hartford, Connecticut, embezzled over a quarter of a million dollars from her workplace and was made to serve jail time, repay the money she stole, and write a letter of apology to her former employer. A Miami man who showed sexually explicit videos of his underage former girlfriend was convicted of child abuse and required to write her a letter of apology. This kind of apology letter writing is commonly mandated by sentencing judges, and the letters are stipulated for lesser and more serious crimes alike.[8]

Another factor in these court-mandated apologies is the highly publicized nature of apologizing on the international stage. Writing in 2004 about the controversy over apologies relating to the treatment of prisoners by the Japanese during World War II, Michael Cunningham states that "the politics of apology have become increasingly prevalent with a growing number of organizations, pressure groups and governments seeking apologies from, or offering apologies to, other agents." Ostensibly seeking reconciliation, governments routinely apologize to their own citizens and each other for various historical injustices. Such apologies have been viewed cynically as "a 'low cost' way for governments to curry favour with marginalized groups, or a manifestation of a trend in society and politics in which confessional and emotional displays are considered laudable." Nonetheless, public apologies are commonly demanded and issued.[9]

Within the framework of restorative justice, a letter of apology is thought to have two effects: it is intended to help rehabilitate the offender and to heal the victim. Taft Lee, writing in the *Yale Law Journal*, describes apologies as favored by judges because of this perceived healing potential.[10] Recall that the essence of restorative justice is aimed at repairing relations that were damaged by the offense while taking into consideration the needs of victims. If such sentences can be said to have a particular hope or desire built into them, it is that sitting down to write such a letter, even if it is required by the court, will bring about genuine self-reflection for the writer, perhaps even catharsis, and that a new state of mind will take shape that results in lasting reform. A well-written apology letter, these legal sentences presume, has the chance to demonstrate that the writer is genuine, malleable, contrite, and otherwise primed for lasting and real rehabilitation.

In an ideal world.

In the real world, court-mandated letters of apology can amount to what are called nonapologies or pseudoapologies: these are "apologies" in name alone that include some combination of being overly vague, passive, minimizing, misdirected, and/or evasive. Writing about nonapologies in public life, Zohar Kampf finds that while "creative forms of apologetic speech" fail to convey key features of conventional apologies, they also allow speakers to "minimize . . . responsibility for misdeeds." This is true in courts of law as well, where apology letters can be deemed inadequate and produce a total rhetorical breakdown: letter writers frequently do not express genuinely apologetic speech and the victims to whom the letters are addressed are not interested in what the offenders have to say. In some cases, the goals of the letter (expressing contrition) are even at odds with the goals of a defendant's legal counsel, who may want to avoid any admission of guilt.[11]

Pennsylvania Supreme Court justice Melvin wrote what her judge deemed a failure or nonapology. It is important to note that she had appealed her conviction, and her attorney had filed to have aspects of her sentence thrown out. The stipulation that the disbarred judge send out photos of herself in handcuffs was rescinded on appeal, but she did not get out of having to write the letters of apology. Melvin had pleaded not guilty in the case, so "counsel for Orie Melvin argued that the obligation to write the apology letters would violate her Fifth Amendment right against self-incrimination." By requiring a written apology, the court was stipulating that she apologize for something she had never admitted doing. So the letters of apology had further legal entanglements. With her appeal rejected by the court, however, the sentencing judge awaited her letters of apology in the fall of 2014.[12]

A November 2014 headline from the *Pennsylvania Record* read: "Orie Melvin's Apology Letters Rejected by Allegheny County Judge." The judge

deemed the letter of apology insufficient, as the letter was devoid of the
markers of a genuine apology. Simply put, she did not take responsibility
in her letter. Aaron Lazare, in his book *On Apology*, cites failing to take
responsibility as one of eight principle failings of nonapologies. The others
include such things as using the passive voice (e.g., "mistakes were made"),
deploying the empathic "I'm sorry" (e.g., "I'm sorry you were hurt"), and
minimizing the offense.[13] Here is the full text of Melvin's nonapology letter:

> October 27, 2014
>
> To the Members of the Pennsylvania Judiciary:
>
> I was accused of misusing my office to assist in my cam-
> paigns for Supreme Court in 2003 and 2009. I plead not
> guilty. I was afforded a trial and I was found guilty. I have
> now exhausted my direct appeal rights. As a matter of law, I
> am guilty of these offenses.
>
> As a condition of my sentence, the judge ordered that I
> write letters of apology to every member of the Pennsylvania
> judiciary and to my former staff members. This has been a
> humiliating experience. It has likewise brought unfathom-
> able distress to my family.
>
> In reflection, I wish I had been more diligent in my super-
> vision of my staff and that I had given them more careful
> instructions with respect to the prohibition on political activ-
> ity set forth in the Supreme Court's Order dated November
> 24, 1998.
>
> I know all of you take pride in the Pennsylvania judiciary
> and that the publicity of my case has had an impact on the
> public's perception of the judiciary. I apologize to you for any
> difficulty it has imposed upon your discharge of your respon-
> sibilities as a judge.
>
> I hope that my case will serve as a cautionary tale to all of
> you.
>
> Sincerely,
> Joan Orie Melvin[14]

A *Pennsylvania Record* article from November 2014 described the former
judge as if she were a student who had failed to properly do her language
arts homework: "Former Supreme Court Justice Joan Orie Melvin has
been ordered back to house arrest while she rewrites court-mandated apology letters to the entire Pennsylvania judiciary." Having determined that

Melvin could put more genuinely apologetic intention into it, Allegheny County judge Lester Nauhaus "ordered Melvin to write personalized letters of apology to each judge in the state, saying the text of a form letter she submitted to the court 'isn't an apology'" and "failed to show any kind of humility." Basic hallmarks of an apology letter—stating such things as "I was wrong" and "I am sorry"—were absent from the letter. In fact, the former judge's letter represents her as unapologetic ("I plead not guilty"), not personally responsible for her crime ("I wish I had been more diligent in my supervision of my staff"), and working to protect her right against self-incrimination. Perhaps she was following the advice of Mary A. De Vries, author of *The New American Handbook of Letter Writing*, who states that "from a legal standpoint, if the matter is truly serious, consult your attorney before committing yourself to writing."[15]

It is worth noting that some in the restorative justice movement have taken exception to the notion of a court-mandated letter of apology because restorative justice advocates insist that apologies need be intrinsically rather than extrinsically motivated for the letter to have any potential meaning for the victims. As one group of restorative justice advocates have written, apology letters "should never be isolated as a quick fix for what the offender did. A parole board member who tells the offender to turn around and apologize to your victim is not helping the offender, and potentially harming the victim." From yet another perspective, letters of apology can do more harm than good. Writing in the *International Journal of Punishment and Sentencing*, David Milward makes the point that "restorative justice may be contrary to the victim's interests by jeopardizing the victim's safety. Acorn points out that domestic abuse often follows patterns of apology (by abuser) and forgiveness (by the victim) that sustain a relationship of power over the victim." In this sense, letters of apology can exacerbate the problem.[16]

In scholarship in the fields of discourse analysis and political theory that focuses on nonapologies, there is no shortage of examples in public life. Nonapologies like the one Melvin submitted are a "common device for image restoration." This is to say that a nonapology still does some work. In Robert Eisinger's study of "thirty-two individual cases of formal congressional disciplinary action in the 20th century . . . eleven congressmen (34.4%) gave non-apologies. Nineteen (59.4%) either denied the charges or did not apologize; and only two (6.3%) offered apologies that fulfilled the definition of an apology." Eisinger found that "of the eleven members of Congress who gave a non-apology, nine ran for re-election, and four of the nine (44.4%) won re-election." It pays not to apologize when you apologize. Nonapologies,

Eisinger argues, are prevalent because they "potentially restore the reputation of the accused" while never truly apologizing.[17]

Scholars do not have a lock on the rhetoric of apology letters, as there is also a widely available popular literature about how to write effective and convincing letters of apology. I mention this to make the point that it is not as if crafting a proper apology would have been too difficult or arcane a task for a judge such as Melvin to accomplish. She could have consulted *Webster's New World Letter Writing Handbook,* for instance, and found that she needed merely to "recall a specific incident" for which the apology is directed. There are dozens of similar online resources describing how to write a proper letter of apology: Wikihow breaks the process down into fifteen steps, the second of which is to "say what you're apologizing for and why it was wrong." Apologyletters.net suggests that "sincerity is the key to writing a good apology letter, and if you don't have that then your missive will come across as more of a letter of obligation." Melvin's apology was, by these definitions, doomed to be seen as unapologetic.[18]

The use of mandated apology letters is curious, in courts of law, because of the way these written documents are used as if they are clear windows into the apologetic or unapologetic souls of the convicted. But as pieces of writing, these "windows" can be either flawed or falsified performances on behalf of the writer. When a judge requires a letter of apology as part of a legal sentence, there is assumed to be an unbroken link between having genuine remorse and having the rhetorical ability to craft a sufficiently remorseful and apologetic written apology. Remorse, contrition, regret, understanding— these are internal states of being that the restorative justice model would very much like every convicted person to have, and written apology letters are used to search for and measure these internal dispositions. Because genuine remorse, contrition, regret, and understanding are nearly impossible to access with absolute certainty, apology letters have been put to use as if they were versions of a polygraph tuned to test for apologetic-ness. And as we saw in the case of former justice Joan Orie Melvin, her "true self" was something she and her legal team were eager to keep hidden.

COURT-MANDATED ESSAYS

Thus far, I have focused on court-mandated letters of apologies, but court-mandated essay writing is equally widespread. In 2013, Illinois teenager Matthew Herrmann was convicted of battery for placing a noose around the neck of an African American fellow student while shouting racial slurs at him. As part of Herrmann's sentence, the presiding judge required him to write an essay on the history of lynching in the United States and to read the essay aloud in a peacemaking ceremony attended by the victim. These ceremonies are common features of restorative justice and used widely in courts and schools that operate under this framework. Instead of concluding that Herrmann was already well-versed in the tradition of lynching in the United States, given the fact that he had deployed a powerful symbol (the noose) taken from the lexicon of American racial oppression, the judge opted to view the crime as the result of his lack of knowledge and understanding. This presumed knowledge deficit, then, would be remedied by the mandatory composition of a short essay. Writing of this kind seems to be seen as capable of inoculating the criminal mind against future deviance.

The *Chicago Tribune* reported that when he "left the courthouse, Herrmann said, 'They didn't give me a word count. I guess I'll just do a three-page, average paper that I would do for school.'"[19] For Herrmann, it was clear that he was being asked by the judge to perform an educational exercise that was familiar to him. By requiring an essay, the judge in the case made the implicit assertion that Herrmann's teachers were in part to blame for the crime since he clearly had not learned enough about American history to cause him to act differently. The judge's sentence would teach him.

Writing about the case for the *Christian Science Monitor*, Laura Edwins described the sentence as "an *unusual* court ruling" in that "Judge James Linn of Cook County, tacked homework onto a probation sentence." In a similar vein, Jason Meisner of the *Chicago Tribune* described Herrmann's sentence as an "*unusual* deal with Cook County prosecutors." These uses of the term *unusual* resonate with the use of the word in the Eighth Amendment to the United States Constitution: "Excessive bail shall not be required, nor excessive fines imposed, nor cruel and *unusual* punishments inflicted" (emphasis added). While this essay-writing sentence was described in the media as unusual, writing-based punishments have actually become quite common. Essay writing has been borrowed from the classroom and employed in the courtroom as a way of insisting that writing-based critical thinking can act as an antidote to criminality.[20]

To give a sense of how common such court-mandated essays are, here are a few recent examples of court cases in which essays have been required by the sentencing judge: In 2007, a man convicted of perjury in Massachusetts was sentenced to write a one-thousand-word essay on the topic of integrity. In 2013, a thirteen-year-old Ohio girl who made a bomb threat at her school was sentenced to write a much shorter "500-word essay on the dangers of false alarms." In the same year, a North Carolina judge required a woman convicted of stealing beer and resisting arrest to write a two-page essay on "How a Lady Should Behave in Public." In all of these cases, essays were meant to fill assumed knowledge deficits—about integrity, false alarms, and "being a lady"—that apparently led to deviance and caused the defendants to wind up in court.[21]

While a court-mandated essay on the topic of integrity may seem a lot like an essay that is required in a classroom, the fact that such essays are required in courtrooms imbues these court-mandated writing tasks with their own forms of significance. When judges require essays they make implicit claims to a relationship between clear, argumentative writing (which is the essence of the essay) that supports a societally approved point of view and lawful behavior. Some crimes, the legal sentences involving essay writing like to imagine, result not from such things as malice or socioeconomic inequality or poverty but from a genuine lack of knowledge. And built into these sentences is the idea that such problems can be quickly remedied in five hundred, one thousand, or five thousand words.

This is evident in the court-mandated essay that another man, Terry Bennett, was required to write on the topic of "the dangers of drugs and their effect on society." Bennett was a thirty-two-year-old convicted cannabis dealer from Bristol, England, who was "ordered by a judge to write a 5,000 word essay." Bennet is also featured in a YouTube video about the punishment, titled "Drug Dealer Made to Write Essay as Punishment." In a 2013 article in the *Mirror*, Bennett is quoted as saying, "It was a shock to be given such an unusual punishment. It's been ages since I last wrote an essay. I asked the judge if I could write a balanced argument for and against cannabis, but he said that since it's illegal, I should only write about the bad things. I'm just going to write about certain dangers caused by cannabis that people might not necessarily know." Judging from these published quotes and other interviews with Bennett that are available online, Bennett is not naive when it comes to the legality of cannabis. But his interest in discussing the complexity of the issue in the form of a "for and against" format was vetoed by the judge. Instead of trying to foster complex thinking on the topic of drugs and society, the judge opted to attempt to indoctrinate Bennet via a one-sided polemical essay.[22]

In court cases in which judges mandate essays, essay writing is used in efforts to rectify what are thought to be particular knowledge deficits that result in criminal behavior. This prompts the question: Do knowledge deficits really lead to crime? And if so, are essays a good way to rectify such knowledge deficits? Nowhere have I found, in the published literature on crime and criminology, evidence that knowledge deficits are a leading cause of crime. Prevailing theories see crime as being driven by such factors as socioeconomic inequality and psychology. And then there are much larger "politics of violence" at work, as described by social theorist Judith Butler. Perhaps because these large-scale factors are nearly impossible to deal with in a single criminal sentence, it is more convenient to see an offender as deficient in a particular kind of knowledge that can be augmented by writing a simple essay. By requiring such an essay, a judge is acting to supplement (at least in part) the presumed work of schools.[23]

THROWING THE BOOK (REPORT) AT THEM

In 2011, when Texas judge John Clinton decided to "throw the book at" several defendants in his court, the book he threw was *The Heart of the Problem*, a self-help text from the 1990s that is described by the publisher as giving "encouragement to everyone who has ever faced a situation that felt insurmountable. By seeking God's answer, even the most complex problems can be solved once and for all." The American Civil Liberties Union of Texas quickly took exception to Judge Clinton's mandatory reading, challenging the legality of requiring defendants to read such overtly religious material. Clinton, a new judge at the time, discontinued the practice of assigning the book while insisting that he had only been "looking for alternative ways to try to get defendants on the right track."[24]

In what have been referred to in the press as "novel sentences," a number of US judges have required defendants in their courts to read books of various kinds and write book reports on them. By requiring such book reports, the judges who pass down such sentences equate criminal behavior with deficits in reading and writing, and the composition of a book report is held up as socially productive behavior. Reading a book and writing a report is not portrayed by these legal sentences as mere busy work; the use of book reports in these cases frames the reports as having real potential to repair the inner workings of those who have run afoul of the law. Reading and writing are set forth as rejuvenating, edifying, healthy activities that just may help turn someone around. This is to say that the use of book reports in such legal sentences directly equates the literate practices of reading and writing with being a participant in the lawful citizenry. Criminals do not read and write, such sentences presume, which is why it is important to read and write about what you read—and through that process, potentially join (or rejoin) the civilized, literate world of readers and writers.

Requiring a religious text in one of these book report–based sentences, as happened in Texas, is not unprecedented. In 2011, a South Carolina woman who caused a car accident and was convicted of drunk driving was sentenced to a prison term and required to write a summary of the Old Testament's the book of Job. And nonreligious book reports have been built into sentences for some pretty serious crimes: In 2012, Otis Mobley Jr. of California was charged with "attempting to sell a grenade launcher to an undercover federal agent" and engaging in a gunfight with law enforcement officers. Federal judge Kandis Westmore ruled that Mobley be released pending trial "with the stipulation that [the defendant] read 'at least one hour every day, and . . . write reports on those books for at least 30 minutes every day.'" In short, the gun-fighting grenade merchant needed to write some book reports to help him better acclimate to law-abiding society. Reuters reported that in Brazil, beginning in 2012, eligible inmates in the nation's prisons became able to shave up to forty-eight days per year off their sentences by reading "up to 12 works of literature, philosophy, science or classics" and writing detailed essays about the books. So the belief in reading and writing extends beyond the United States.[25]

Court-mandated, court-sponsored, and court-approved reading and writing is informed by a very particular point of view about traditional literate practices such as reading a book and writing about it: reading and writing are seen as restorative, nurturing, wholesome, redemptive practices of law-abiding citizens. Note that these are not sentences that require convicted criminals to watch films or television shows, and no one has been sentenced to play a video game. "Read a book," these sentences insist, and the act of doing so will change and reform you. Reading and writing are seen as powerfully edifying. While I have found instances where judges have required that book reports be delivered orally, reading and writing predominate in such legal sentences because of a simple logic and system of beliefs: reading and writing will rectify certain deficits within the individual that lead to crime.

Another implicit assumption of such sentences is that these legal sentences perceive that defendants have shortcomings in the areas of their humanities-based educations in particular (in middle and high school, the humanities are represented by such reading-and-writing-intensive classes as social studies, language arts, and political science). Those who have run afoul of the law do not need to learn about science or practice scientific thinking, these judges imply via sentencing, and nor does anyone who has run afoul of the law need to study art or practice music. Similarly, math will not help. The burden instead falls on reading and writing as redemptive, important activities that will bring defendants to justice.

Requiring writing in a court of law makes a simple statement that not enough reading and writing took place while the defendant was in school. In a court of law where crime is framed as an educational problem, it is a logical conclusion to point the finger at the language arts teachers, who clearly should have assigned more book reports in the first place. When judges "throw the book at" those convicted in their courts in these ways, a lack of reading and writing is both at the heart of the injustice and the solution to the problem.

THE WRITING CURE

All of the mandated writing tasks I have discussed in this chapter—the letters of apology, essays, and book reports—attempt to perform a kind of writing cure. In the case of the unapologetic former justice of the Pennsylvania Supreme Court, the sentencing judge used writing in an effort to peer into the inner workings of the former justice's consciousness, to symbolically break her defiant will, and to ensure that she had apologized to those she had hurt. Of course, the former justice refused to truly apologize in her letters, and in that sense the epistolary punishment failed to achieve its task. But would the writing cure have truly succeeded if the apology letters Melvin wrote had been perfectly and authentically apologetic? Even the most perfectly crafted apology letter might not reflect genuine feeling. In the case of the student who put a noose around the neck of an African American student, writing an essay was used to try to teach the assailant a body of knowledge that, presumably, would have circumvented the crime. In this case, writing was thought to have enough power to neutralize the centuries of racist thinking that informed the attack. In the many other cases I have described, writing is used in efforts to reach and transform convicted criminals in ways that other, more traditional punitive sentences might not be able to. When writing is administered in this way, it is figured as a special cure.

The various ways that mandated writing is currently used in the courts—from court-mandated letters of apology to essays to book reports—are informed by a nostalgic, romantic belief that sitting down to write (above many other things) has a profound and positive effect on a writer. Writing, this perspective suggests, is a tool that can even transform a "bad guy" into a "good guy," creating genuine reform within the mind and soul of the writer. Writing is used to recalibrate, redirect, and reeducate those who have done wrong, turning them (or so the logic goes) into members of the law-abiding, literate citizenry. When seen in this way, writing is a sort of supertechnology, capable of much more than merely expressing and recording ideas. Readers and writers are people who do good, these court sentences presume, and writing works back on writers while they write on the page.

So what of those who are found guilty in a court of law but cannot read and write, so cannot enjoy (if that is the right word) a writing-based sentence? Having to write a letter of apology, an essay, or a book report—these are all clearly sentences passed down to defendants who are seen as capable of such tasks. In a clear sense, there is privilege for those who can read and write built into these sentences, as in some cases tangible benefits—such as release pending trial—are granted in exchange for reading-and-writing tasks. There is also a privileged assumption in all such sentences that literate acts are integral to contrition, repairing relationships (via letters of apology), and rehabilitation. If you cannot read and write, you clearly cannot accomplish the goals set out as valuable by such sentences. Writing-based legal sentences absolutely position those who can write as more likely to be redeemable via court-mandated reading and writing. Phrased in the most basic way possible, writing-based legal sentences suggest that literate criminals have more promise for reform than people who cannot read and write.

As we have seen in this chapter and in the rest of this book, writing is frequently turned to as a disciplinary technology that is imagined to have great powers. The sheer abundance of writing-based legal sentences both reflects and reifies beliefs in writing as transformative and powerful. Writing can change you, these sentences assert. It can also improve you, break you, and rehabilitate you.

CONCLUSION

Seeing Writing in a Dim Light

The art of punishing, then, must rest on a whole technology of representation.
—Michel Foucault, *Discipline and Punish*

M any of the ways that I have described writing being used as punishment have been condemned at one point or another, and those that have not surely could be. There is a long history of critiquing the use of writing as punishment in schools. While the use of sign shaming has grown in popularity in recent years in the United States, China banned shame parades in 2010, and US newspapers in the 1930s represented the practice as appalling when they reported on Nazis who forced Jews to wear signs and parade through city streets. And while drunk shaming seems to some like just another party game, it has come under scrutiny due to some instances of it being coupled with sexual assault and even death. Forced tattooing has also been criminalized and condemned, as it appeals to sex traffickers precisely because it degrades the recipients of the tattoos and diminishes their self-determination. The final form of writing-based punishment I discussed in this book—instances of judges requiring mandated apology letters, essays, and book reports—is problematic in that it privileges written literacy while ignoring some deep-seated causes of crime. So it would seem to make sense in a book such as this one to conclude with a broad condemnation of writing as punishment.

But my purpose in this book has not been to rail against these punishments and shaming rituals, even though all of them are somewhat warped and some are just plain evil. Instead, my principle goal has been to reveal the roles writing has in what Foucault calls "the art of punishing."[1] One reason I am not simply "against" most of these uses of writing as punishment is because I see them all as products of the cultures, situations, circumstances, and beliefs that foster them. Sign shaming appealed to the Nazis in the 1930s for some of the same reasons it appeals to judges now—but banning the practice of sign shaming would no more change our current shame-hungry society than such a ban would have magically altered Nazi Germany and circumvented the Holocaust. Similarly, forced tattooing within the domain of sex trafficking is insidious, but it is part and parcel of much larger systems of exploitation. It is the causes of writing-based punishments that should be scrutinized, I think, as opposed to simply banning various ways that writing is used as punishment.

Even more importantly, I see the vernacular uses of writing described in this book as cultural practices that display the workings of otherwise hidden values and beliefs about writing. The uses of writing as punishment described in this book tell a story about how people in various walks of life in contemporary US society see writing as a productive tool for enacting everything from discipline to reform to subordination. The story about what writing is capable of is most often told as a positive narrative about the values of writing and literacy, but the many ways writing is used as punishment complicates such a one-sided perspective. To argue for the end of the writing-based punishments described in this book would be to campaign to extinguish evidence of some very revealing cultural beliefs about writing.

Furthermore, keep in mind that those who are punished with writing often find ways to resist their punishments. Children find workarounds when they have to write lines in school, defendants refuse to genuinely apologize, and those who are made to hold signs in public sometimes wear dark glasses to hide their faces from public view. The students I spoke with about drunk shaming reminded me that waking up in the morning with writing all over your body can be quickly remedied by a hot shower and some soap, and even forcibly applied tattoos can be covered over and removed (in some cases). The uses of writing as punishment that I have described can certainly be palpably humiliating and real. However, most writing-based punishments have at least the potential to be resisted, ignored, and made light of. The messages people are compelled to write down for punishment are much like the words and phrases that others are made to hold, wear, and physically embody: in some cases, all of these writing-based punishments do not always get inscribed in the minds of the writers or become permanently affixed to their identities in some way.

So why, if writing-based punishments have the known potential to be weak and resistible, is writing used to shame and humiliate across so many domains in modern life? All of the different forms of writing-based punishments that I have described in this book come out of very different environments, situations, and circumstances. And keep in mind that when different people use writing as punishment, they draw from varied histories and exist in disparate worlds. So teachers who use writing as punishment do so based on traditions embedded in teaching and learning, and judges who use it act based on developments in jurisprudence. But there are some shared beliefs about writing that cut across all of these domains and construe writing as a simple, appealing tool for punishment. While the contexts of punishment writing vary, writing is used in all of these scenes because of a shared set of beliefs about what writing is good for and capable of. If it were not for these shared beliefs, other modes of expression would be used instead of writing. The beliefs, as I have identified them, are that writing is seen as having transformative powers, as a tool of authentic expression, and as being able to thoroughly represent (speak for) a person who is affiliated with a text.

These three beliefs about writing are not aberrant or relegated exclusively to the use of writing as punishment. Far from it. Instead, they prompt me and other teachers to regularly assign writing in our classes, work with students on their writing, and generally value written communication. These beliefs are why some of us keep written journals, write a note or letter when we want to express something special to someone, and even part of why we wear T-shirts with writing on them. Many uses of writing stem from seeing writing as transformative, authentic, and/or representative of a writer's true thoughts and beliefs. My point here is to insist that the uses of writing as punishment that I have described in this book are not based on aberrant, entirely deviant perspectives about what writing is capable of. Instead, the beliefs that ground the use of writing as punishment are widely held, affirmed, and accepted notions about the power and importance of writing. This is part of why various forms of punishment writing have been so long-standing and invulnerable to critique. Writing-based punishments are not based upon unusual views about writing that can be easily dismissed or done away with. Instead, the perceived value of punishment writing is perpetually renewed by teachers like me every time we assign writing in our classes. Using writing to punish and to teach have their differences, but both uses of writing are rooted in many of the same beliefs about what writing is thought to be capable of. This study of the use of writing as punishment provides an occasion to rethink and question some core beliefs about writing.

It is almost unfathomable that writing-based punishments have been used in efforts to curb both classroom gum chewing and campus rape. Equally surprising is that dog-shaming images rely on the same rhetorical mechanisms used in shame parades orchestrated by judges and parents.

But the use of writing to discipline and shame such disparate offenders makes sense if you think of these punishments not only as ways to curb certain behaviors but as a "technology of representation." For Foucault, punishments are larger meaning-making systems and a "complex of signs" that produce social meaning. The use of writing-based punishments of all kinds represents acts of writing and written language as, more than anything else, consequential, and in this way the many uses of writing as punishment both come from and prop up larger cultural beliefs in the value and importance of writing.[2]

The many uses of writing I have discussed in this book have certain patterns to them: particular forms of writing are used to alter individuals, often with the participation of readers and other onlookers. It can be easy to think of writing as merely a recording tool, or simply a tool for expressing complex ideas, or as one of many means of interpersonal communication. Writing is all of these things. But it is also presumed by many to have special affordances that can be accessed through ritualized uses of writing as punishment. For over a century, the teachers who use writing as punishment have crafted particular writing-based rituals to exploit these discipline-based affordances of writing, and the many other actors described in this book have followed suit. Considered side by side, these various punishments express a great deal of faith in the powers of writing but at the same time equal belief in its capabilities as a dark art.

NOTES

Introduction

1. Quotations: Knoblauch (2011, 245); Autrey (1991, 74); Ong (1982). On the positive view of writing, see CWPA, NCTE, and NWP (2011); Alexander (2011); Duffy (2017); Rose (1990); Danielewicz (2008); CWPA (2014); Bowden (1995); and Branch (1998).

2. Tyre (2012); CWPA (2014).

3. There is a substantial body of scholarship theorizing the notion of shame. See Sigmund Freud's *Interpretation of Dreams* (1900); Silvan Tomkins's work in Sedgwick and Frank's *Shame and Its Sisters* (1995a); and Sedgwick and Frank's "Shame in the Cybernetic Fold" (1995b). For an exploration of the erotics of humiliation, see Wayne Koestenbaum's *Humiliation* (2011).

4. Book (1999).

5. Baron (2012).

Chapter 1

1. Hogan (1985).

2. Gibson (2014); Duffy (2017).

3. On literacy and good citizenship, see Wan (2011); on writing leading to success, see Simonds (2013) and Leibowitz (2016); and on literacy and higher-level reasoning, see Ong (1982).

4. Alexander (2006, 29).

5. Anonymous (1898, 417); Rawlings (2016); Rubin v. Lafayette Parish School Board (1995); Spillett (2014); Tan (2016).

6. Brodkey (1987, 400).

7. Laidlaw (2013).

8. For the study on writing unfamiliar words, see Conway and Gathercole (1989); on students writing about and remembering more on subjects that interested them, see Klein and Boals (2001); on notetaking, see Mueller and Oppenheimer (2014).

9. Reflective writing in particular has grown in popularity in recent years as a go-to mode of punishment writing, as advocates of restorative justice promote writing about feelings and motivations (Gardner 2016, 55). In chapter 2, I return to justifications for punishment writing in the restorative justice framework, as

restorative justice is popular not only in schools but in some courts of law.

10. Arkansas Department of Human Services v. Caldwell (1992).

11. Friedersdorf (2018); quote in Herzog (2018).

12. Ellis v. Cleveland Municipal School District (2006); B. V. v. Department of Education, State of Hawaii (2005).

13. Bryce (1868, 605).

14. Romanes (1879, 789); Churchill (1885, 78).

15. Dukes (1893, 22).

16. Hogan (1985, 41).

17. NCTE (1984).

18. Gibson (2014, 16–19); Duffy (2017, 229, 230).

19. UK Department for Education (2016, 9).

20. Owen (2014).

Chapter 2

1. Jacobs (2010).

2. On shaming in legal literature, see Rodogno (2009); Kahan and Posner (1999); and Nussbaum (2004). Quote by Goldman (2015, 417).

3. Perhaps the most blatant examples of mandated speech, though not in written form, have involved hostages and prisoners of war who have been made to espouse propaganda for their captors. Laura Hillenbrand describes an example of this in her book *Unbroken: A World War II Story of Survival, Resilience, and Redemption.* In Hillenbrand's account of Louis Zamperini's experiences as a prisoner of war in Japan, she describes how he was compelled to propagandize for the Japanese over the radio. Many other examples of hostages being made to propagandize for their captors exist. Being forced to write a letter of apology (of the kind discussed later in the book) is another form of mandated speech in that such letters are often written against the will of the author.

4. Koestenbaum (2011, 70).

5. Fox (2014, 338).

6. For Italian woman, see McGough (2006, 220); for domestic abuser, see Wipper (1988, 411–12).

7. Book (1999).

8. Edge (2009, 9–10); Keyes (2010, chapter 3, page 1).

9. Berson (2013, 133–45).

10. US Holocaust Memorial Museum (n.d.).

11. Translations are by translator Erik Macki, http://www.seanet.com/~macki.

12. Fifth Estate Collective (1977).

13. Matthäus and Roseman (2009, 282); Grunberger (1995, 81).

14. Book (1999, 654).

15. United States v. Gementera (2004); Goldman (2015).

16. Nussbaum (2004, 233, 230–37).

17. Ferrise (2014); Morris (2012); Ross (2015); Daily Mail Reporter (2009).

18. Koestenbaum (2011, 92).

19. Shame parades are not the only way that speech has been legally mandated. Laws have been passed, for instance, requiring agencies such as health clinics to provide particular kinds of information to their patients (California Assembly 2015).

20. Goldman (2015, 417).

21. For the North Carolina punishment, see Clarke (2012); for Florida, see Daily Mail Reporter (2012a).

22. For California incident, see Associated Press (2007); for Texas, see Daily Mail Reporter (2013); for Miami, see Belkin (2012).

23. For sign holding in Miami, see "I Like to Steal" (2012); in North Carolina, see "Michael Bell, Jr." (2012); in Illinois, see "Teen Forced" (2012); for twerking, see Boone (2013).

24. For Facebook post from Ohio, see Cohen (2014); for post on Hailey, see Angry-CommGuy (2013); for post from Houston mother, see Bershad (2012). The mother who compelled her daughter to post the image of herself holding a sign that read "Since I want to post photos of me holding liquor . . ." is the widely published author ReShonda Tate Billingsley. Billingsley has discussed this punishment in various interviews and published a justification of her approach at http://mybrownbaby.com/2012/05/tough-love-on-social-media-reshonda-tate-billingsleys-old-school-parenting-in-the-new-millennium.

25. Garfinkel (1956, 424).

Chapter 3

1. La Ganga and Mather (2013); Davies (2013); Burleigh (2013); Salonga (2013). The tragic case of Audrie Pott had striking similarities to two other stories in the news in 2013. Earlier in the year, in Steubenville, Ohio, two teens had been convicted of raping a young girl at a party; after the assault, the assailants posted images and video of the attack online (Oppel 2013). And then in May 2013, three Chicago teens were charged with sexually assaulting a twelve-year-old girl. Similarly, videos of the attack were posted to Facebook (Jauregui 2013).

2. For the Colorado case, see Denver Channel (2014); for Texas, see S. Smith (2007); for court cases, see Martin Gump v. William Walker Jr. (2005); David Coombs v. J. B. Hunt Transport (2012).

3. Leong (2015); Mithal (2004, 39).

4. Vandervort (2013, 143).

5. Pritchard and Russo (2010). The term "drunken buckaroo" refers to a children's game called "Buckaroo" that involves stacking objects on a bucking miniature horse. In the party game, the victim has things like cups or bottles stacked on him or her.

6. My small study of attitudes and beliefs about drunk shaming was approved by my campus research board in 2014: IRB Protocol Number 15250. I recruited student participants by describing my research to students in a large campus lecture

course. In all, fifteen students agreed to participate, and I met with the participants in two groups. I led focus-group style discussions that lasted approximately
thirty minutes each, and I attempted to facilitate organic, free-ranging conversations with the students on the topic of drunk shaming. I started each focus group
by asking the participants: "Show of hands: Have any of you ever seen someone
pass out at a party because he or she drank too much?" then gradually moved to
asking if they had witnessed or knew about the practice of passed-out partiers
getting written on. As much as possible, I encouraged students to respond to one
another in the discussions. The anonymity of the participants was maintained and
they were each paid twenty dollars for their involvement in the study.

7. Detel (2013, 91); Ronson (2015, 68–78).

8. Copeland (2005).

9. Delaney (2008, 101–3).

10. Delaney (2008, 99).

11. Of this group of online media sites, CollegeHumor.com, which was established online in 1999, is the most well-known: the site features images, videos,
and accounts both created by the in-house staff and posted by users (www.
collegehumor.com/static/about). It is worth noting that, online, many separate
media sites can be owned by a single parent company, thus only creating an
illusion that a diverse array of online entities host similar content. In this case,
at least two of these sites are owned by different online media conglomerates:
CollegeHumor.com is owned by parent company InterActiveCorp (which owns
such media sites as Vimeo and ask.com), and online media conglomerate EVTV1
owns dailyhaha.com.

12. Workman (2001); Delaney (2008, 116).

13. Workman (2001, 429).

14. Armstrong, Hamilton, Armstrong, and Seeley (2014, 100).

15. Simpson (2006).

16. Mithal (2004, 40).

Chapter 4

1. United States v. Campbell (2014); Kirkland (2009, 375).

2. Sweeney (2012); Kirkland (2009, 376); Johnson (2016, 231).

3. Shontavia Johnson (2016) explores the connection between the forced tattooing of slaves and legal trademarks because of the contemporary rise in "skin-
vertising," which is the voluntary acquisition of tattoos that feature trademarked
symbols, icons, and phrases. Koeller (2015).

4. Pew Research Center (2008).

5. On criminals and slaves being tattooed, see Stewart (2014); for Japanese criminals, see Ashcroft (2016).

6. Davis (1988, 49); Mayor (1999, 55); Kamen (2013, 11).

7. Johnson (2016, 231).

8. Perhaps the most comprehensive repository for images of tattoos applied by

the Nazis in Auschwitz is available online via the US Holocaust Memorial Museum. Simply search for "tattoo" at www.ushmm.org to see hundreds of historical photographs. US Holocaust Memorial Museum (n.d.); Rosenthal (n.d.); Black (2008).

9. Forcibly applied animal brands for the purpose of labeling animals as property have an even longer history than human brands and forced tattoos, with animal brands (applied with hot metal) having been used in "most ancient civilizations." Blancou (2001, 420).

10. US Code (2011); US Department of State (n.d.); Walker-Rodriguez and Hill (2011).

11. Kristof (2012); International Labour Office (2012).

12. Gayle (2014).

13. Fisher quote from Ruta, dir. (2014); for San Diego incident, see Sharma (2011); in the Miami incident, the trafficker's nickname "Suave" was tattooed on one eyelid and "house" on the other (Kuruvilla 2013); for Texas incident, see Robert Lee Menyweather v. State of Texas (2014); for California incidents, see People v. Jerron Callahan (2009) and Appleton (2015); on barcodes, see Associated Press (2017).

14. Daily Mail Reporter (2012b).

15. Kelly (2014); Music Intern (2015).

16. Associated Press (2006).

17. On Steven Jiminez, see Fuller (2010); on Singapore incident, see Anonymous (2009); for gang tattooing, see People v. Dale J. Jung (1999); for cat incident, see Kenny (2014).

18. Kelly (2014).

19. www.ink180.com; Taylor (2015).

Chapter 5

1. Gilchriese (2015); for UC Berkeley case, see Sofie Karasek v. Regents of the University of California (2015); for Wheaton College, see Gutowski and St. Clair (2017); for *Hunting Ground*, see Dick (2012); "Biennial Report on Alcohol" (2014).

2. Meisner (2013); Grise (2013); Nazaryan (2012); Kannanl (2012); "Woman Sentenced to Write" (2014); Annanova (2013); Fraley (2012).

3. Foucault (1977, 7).

4. Kant (1796); Bentham (1823); Hart cited in Koritansky (2011, 2).

5. For direct practical reparation, see Bageric (2001); for apology letters, see Hill (2008, 57, 59).

6. V. Taft (2015); Valiente (2015).

7. Commonwealth of Pennsylvania v. Joan Orie Melvin (2013).

8. It is worth noting that apologies also appear at another stage of legal proceedings: the allocution. Allocution is the opportunity for the defendant to speak before sentencing, and it is common for people to use a letter to state their remorse (often in the interest of a lesser sentence). Gruber (2014); for Nashau, NH, case, see Shalhoup (2015); for Canyon City, CO, case, see "Cops and Courts" (2015); for Hartford,

CT, case, see Pederson (2015); for Miami case, see Ovalle (2015).

9. Cunningham (2004, 561); Blatz, Schumann, and Ross (2009); Weyeneth (2001).

10. Lee (2000).

11. In 2013, the same year as Melvin's conviction, the state of Pennsylvania passed the Benevolent Gesture Medical Professional Liability Act, which allows health-care providers to apologize to their patients without the apologies being used later as admissions of guilt. Such protections do not extend beyond health-care providers, however. Lazare (2003, 99–100); Zohar Kampf (2009, 2258).

12. Campisi (2013).

13. Lazare (2003, 8–9).

14. Bonner (2014).

15. Mandak (2015); Boyle (2014); De Vries (2000, 253).

16. Seymour, English, and Weston (2001); Milward (2008, 78).

17. Kampf (2009, 2258); Eisinger (2011).

18. Bly (2004, 63); "How to Write an Apology Letter" (n.d.); "How Not to Write an Apology" (n.d.).

19. Meisner (2013).

20. Edwins (2013, emphasis added); Meisner (2013, emphasis added).

21. For Massachusetts sentence, see Murray (2007); for Ohio sentence, see Read (2013); for North Carolina sentence, see Hansen (2013).

22. R. Smith (2013).

23. On socioeconomic inequality, see Blau and Blau (1982); on psychology, see Hollin (2013); Butler (1994).

24. Brandt and Skinner (1996); "Judge's Sentence" (2011); Miller (2011).

25. For South Carolina case, see "Judge Demands" (2012); for California, see Nazaryan (2012); for Brazil, see Murphy (2012).

Conclusion

1. Foucault (1977, 104).

2. Foucault (1977, 104, 106).

WORKS CITED

Alexander, Jeffrey. 2006. "Cultural Pragmatics: Social Performance between Ritual and Strategy." In *Social Performance: Symbolic Action, Cultural Pragmatics, and Ritual,* edited by Jeffrey C. Alexander, Bernhard Giesen, and Jason L. Mast, 29–90. London: Cambridge University Press.

Alexander, Kara Poe. 2011. "Success, Victims, and Prodigies: 'Master' and 'Little' Cultural Narratives in the Literacy Narrative Genre." *College Composition and Communication* 62 (4): 608–33.

AngryCommGuy. 2013. "Mom Catches Daughter Cyber-Bullying." https://www.reddit.com/r/pics/comments/1uhfq8/mom_catches_daughter_cyberbullying.

Annanova. 2013. "Man Made to Write Lines for Stealing Nude Portrait." *Police Oracle,* December 14, 2013. http://www.policeoracle.com/quirkie/quirkie/2013/Dec/14/Man-made-to-write-lines-for-stealing-nude-portrait_75775.html.

Anonymous. 1898. "Punishments." *Public School Magazine,* 415–19.

Anonymous. 2009. "Singapore Tattooist Jailed for Disfiguring Woman." *Two Circles,* March 19, 2009. http://twocircles.net/2009mar19/singapore_tattooist_jailed_disfiguring_woman.html#.WD3iKNzggwJ.

Appleton, Rory. 2015. "Two Fresno Men Plead Guilty to Sex Trafficking Teenage Girls." *Fresno Bee,* May 7, 2015. http://www.fresnobee.com/news/local/crime/article20945295.html.

Arkansas Department of Human Services v. Caldwell. 1992. No. CA 91-296. Court of Appeals of Arkansas, Division II. https://scholar.google.com/scholar_case?-case=2741130233207653560&q=%22write+a+report%22+teacher&hl=en&as_sdt=400006.

Armstrong, Elizabeth A., Laura T. Hamilton, Elizabeth M. Armstrong, and J. Lotus Seeley. 2014. "'Good Girls': Gender, Social Class, and Slut Discourse on Campus." *Social Psychology Quarterly* 77 (2): 100–122.

Ashcroft, Brian. 2016. *Japanese Tattoos: History, Culture, Design.* North Clarendon, VT: Tuttle Publishing.

Associated Press. 2006. "Indiana Inmate Tattoos Face with Child Victim's Name: 'Katie's Revenge.'" *Fox News,* September 28. http://www.foxnews.com/story/2006/09/28/indiana-inmate-tattoos-face-with-child-victim-name-katie-revenge.html.

———. 2007. "Here's Your Sign: Teen Gets Public Punishment." *NBC News,* May

17. http://www.nbcnews.com/id/18729564/ns/us_news-life/t/heres-your-sign-teen-gets-public-punishment/#.VPYGAlPF-gE.

———. 2017. "Woman Sentenced for Trafficking Teen Tattooed with Bar Code." *New York Post*, December 6. https://nypost.com/2017/12/06/woman-sentenced-for-trafficking-teen-tattooed-with-bar-code.

Autrey, Ken. 1991. "Toward a Rhetoric of Journal Writing." *Rhetoric Review* 10 (1): 74–90.

Bageric, Mirko. 2001. *Punishment and Sentencing.* New York: Routledge-Cavendish.

Baron, Dennis. 2012. *A Better Pencil: Readers, Writers, and the Digital Revolution.* Oxford: Oxford University Press.

Belkin, Lisa. 2012. "Humiliating Children in Public: A New Parenting Trend?" *Huffington Post*, April 18. http://www.huffingtonpost.com/lisa-belkin/humiliating-children-to-teach-them-_b_1435315.html.

Bentham, Jeremy. 1823. *An Introduction to the Principles of Morals and Legislation.* http://oll.libertyfund.org/titles/bentham-an-introduction-to-the-principles-of-morals-and-legislation.

Bershad, Jon. 2012. "Is Social Media Humiliation a Good Way for Modern Parents to Punish Their Children?" *Mediaite*, May 9. http://www.mediaite.com/online/is-social-media-humiliation-a-good-way-for-modern-parents-to-punish-their-children.

Berson, Joel S. 2013. "On the Trail of the Scarlet AD." *Nathaniel Hawthorne Review* 39 (1): 133–54.

"Biennial Report on Alcohol and Other Drug Efforts 2012–2013 and 2013–2014 Academic Years." 2014. University of Illinois. http://odos.illinois.edu/downloads/AODO_Biennial_Report.pdf.

Billingsley, ReShonda Tate. 2012. "Old School Parenting in the New Millennium." Mybrownbaby.com. http://mybrownbaby.com/2012/05/tough-love-on-social-media-reshonda-tate-billingsleys-old-school-parenting-in-the-new-millennium.

Black, Edwin. 2008. *IBM and the Holocaust: The Strategic Alliance between Nazi Germany and America's Most Powerful Corporation.* Westport, CT: Dialogue Press.

Black, Rebecca (Performer). 2013. "Saturday" music video. https://www.youtube.com/watch?v=GVCzdpagXOQ&list=RDGVCzdpagXOQ.

Blancou, J. 2001. "A History of the Traceability of Animals and Animal Products." *Revue Scientifique et Technique* 20 (2): 420–25.

Blatz, Craig W., Karina Schumann, and Michael Ross. 2009. "Government Apologies for Historical Injustices." *Political Psychology* 30 (2): 219–41.

Blau, Judith R., and Peter M. Blau. 1982. "The Cost of Inequality: Metropolitan Structure and Violent Crime." *American Sociological Review* 47 (1): 114–29.

Bly, Robert W. 2004. *Webster's New World Letter Writing Handbook.* Indianapolis: Wiley Publishing.

Bonner, Teresa. 2014. "Read Joan Orie Melvin's Apology Letter." Pennlive. http://www.pennlive.com/midstate/index.ssf/2014/10/read_joan_orie_melvins_apology.html.

Book, Aaron S. 1999. "Shame on You: An Analysis of Modern Shame Punishment as an Alternative to Incarceration." *William and Mary Law Review* 40 (2): 653–86. http://scholarship.law.wm.edu/wmlr/vol40/ iss2/8.

Boone, John. 2013. "Mother Publicly Shames 11-Year-Old Daughter for Twerking at a School Dance, Forces Her to Apologize." *E! Online*, September 10. http://www.eonline.com/news/457429/mother-publicly-shames-11-year-old-daughter-for-twerking-at-a-school-dance-forces-her-to-apologize.

Bowden, Darsie. 1995. "The Rise of a Metaphor: 'Voice' in Composition Pedagogy." *Rhetoric Review* 14 (1): 173–88.

Boyle, Jim. 2014. "Orie Melvin's Apology Letters Rejected by Allegheny County Judge." *Pennsylvania Record.* http://pennrecord.com/news/15052-orie-melvins-apology-letters-rejected-by-allegheny-county-judge.

Braff, Zach, dir. 2004. *Garden State.* Century City, CA: Fox Searchlight Pictures.

Branch, Kirk. 1998. "From the Margins at the Center: Literacy, Authority, and the Great Divide." *College Composition and Communication* 50 (2): 206–31.

Brandt, Henry, and Kerry L. Skinner. 1996. *How to Stop Coping and Find the Cure for Your Struggle.* Paris, ON: B and H Publishing Group.

Brodkey, Linda. 1987. "Modernism and the Scene(s) of Writing." *College English* 49 (4): 396–418.

Bryce, J. 1868. "General Report on the County of Lancaster." In *Reports from Commissioners: Twenty-Four Volumes.* Schools Inquiry Commission, Northern Counties. https://play.google.com/books/reader?id=gzMIAAAAQAAJ&prinsec=frontcover&output=reader&hl=en&pg=GBS.PP1.

Burleigh, Nina. 2013. "Sexting, Shame and Suicide: A Shocking Tale of Sexual Assault in the Digital Age." *Rolling Stone*, September 17. http://www.rollinstone.com/culture/news/sexting-shame-and-suicide-20130917.

Butler, Judith. 1994. *The Postmodern Turn: New Perspectives on Social Theory.* Cambridge: Cambridge University Press.

B. V. v. Department of Education, State of Hawaii. 2005. Civil No. 05-00116 JMS. United States District Court, D. Hawaii. https://scholar.google.com/scholar_case?case=6479351424528532989&q=%22name+on+the+board%22&hl=en&as_sdt=400006.

California Assembly. 2012. Bill No. 1956, Chapter 746. http://leginfo.legislature.ca.gov/faces/billNavClient.xhtml?bill_id=201120120AB1956.

———. 2015. Bill No. 775. http://www.legtrack.com/bills/leginfo.public.ca.gov/pub/15-16/bill/asm/ab_0751-0800/ab_775_bill_20151009_chaptered.htm.

Campisi, Jon. 2013. "Pa. Superior Court Stays Apology Letter-Writing Portion of Orie Melvin's Sentence." *Pennsylvania Record.* http://pennrecord.com/news/12002-pa-superior-court-stays-apology-letter-writing-portion-of-orie-melvins-sentence.

Churchill, Frederick. 1885. "High-Pressure Education." *Medical Times and Gazette,* no. 1803, 76–78. https://books.google.com/books?id=n_NEimVTHvoC&pg=PA78&dq=%22writing+lines%22+punishment&hl=en&sa=X&ved

=0ahUKEwjLnNfy4a_MAhWIr4MKHfUVDLMQ6AEILTAD#v=onepage&q
=%22writing%20lines%22%20punishment&f=false.

Clarke, Suzan. 2012. "'Disrespectful' Teen Made to Carry Sign along Busy
    Road." *ABC News*, April 29. http://abcnews.go.com/blogs/headlines/2012/04/
    disrespectful-teen-made-to-carry-sign-along-busy-road.

Cohen, David. 2012. "Mom Disciplines Daughter with Humiliating Facebook
    Timeline Cover Image." *Social Times*. http://www.adweek.com/socialtimes/
    cover-image-discipline/390443.

Commonwealth of Pennsylvania v. Joan Orie Melvin. 2013. Docket No. CP-02-CR-
    0009885-2012. http://www.pacourts.us/assets/opinions/Superior/out/844WDA
    2013o%20-%201016093901793243.pdf.

Conway, Martin A., and Susan E. Gathercole. 1989. "Writing and Long-Term Mem-
    ory: Evidence for a 'Translation' Hypothesis." *Quarterly Journal of Experimental
    Psychology* 42 (3): 513–27.

Coombs, David, v. J. B. Hunt Transport. 2012. No. CA 11-517. Court of Appeals of
    Arkansas. https://scholar.google.com/scholar_case?case=3198045976254505&q=
    %22wrote+on+his+body%22&hl=en&as_sdt=400006.

Copeland, Libby. 2005. "Sleeping It Off? Shmile for the Birdy! For 'Drunk
    Shamers,' No Gutter Is Sacred." *Washington Post*, January 16. http://www.
    washingtonpost.com/wp-dyn/articles/A12747-2005Jan15.html.

"Cops and Courts." 2015. *Blue Mountain Eagle*, January 13. http://www.
    bluemountaineagle.com/Local_News/20150113/cops-courts.

Cunningham, Michael. 2004. "Prisoners of the Japanese and the Politics of Apology:
    A Battle over History and Memory." *Journal of Contemporary History* 39 (4): 561–74.

CWPA (Council of Writing Program Administrators). 2014. "WPA Outcomes
    Statement for First-Year Composition (3.0)." http://wpacouncil.org/positions/
    outcomes.html.

CWPA, NCTE, and NWP (Council of Writing Program Administrators, National
    Council of Teachers of English, and National Writers Project). 2011. *Framework
    for Success in Postsecondary Writing*. WPA Council. http://wpacouncil.org/files/
    framework-for-success-postsecondary-writing.pdf.

Daily Mail Reporter. 2009. "Women Who Stole Gift Cards from Birthday Girl, 9,
    Hold Signs of Shame in Town Centre." *Daily Mail*, November 5. http://www.
    breakingworldnewstoday.com/2014/03/b2622.html.

———. 2012a. "'I Sneak Boys in at 3am and Disrespect My Parents': Girl, 15,
    Forced to Stand by Side of the Road with Humiliating Sign." *Daily Mail*, Novem-
    ber 22. http://www.dailymail.co.uk/news/article-2237221/Girl-15-forced-stand-
    road-humiliating-sign.html.

———. 2012b. "Pimps Tattooed BAR CODE on Wrist of Woman Imprisoned,
    Whipped and Forced to Work as a Prostitute." *Daily Mail*, March 25. http://www.
    dailymail.co.uk/news/article-2120110/Spanish-police-investigating-Madrid-
    prostitution-ring-free-woman-19-ownership-tattoo-wrist.html.

————. 2013. "'Honk If You Hate Bullies!' Father Makes Son Hold Sign for Bullying Student." *Daily Mail*, October 4. http://www.dailymail.co.uk/news
/article-2443814/Honk-hate-bullies-Father-makes-son-hold-sign-bullying-
student.html.

Danielewicz, Jane. 2008. "Personal Genres, Public Voices." *College Composition and
Communication* 59 (3): 420–50.

Davies, Katie. 2013. "'**** Was Here': Teen Sex-Attackers Wrote Crude Messages
on Audrie Pott's Naked Body with a Marker and Photographed Them after Sexual Assault." *Daily Mail*, April 16. http://www.dailymail.co.uk/news
/article-2309945/Audrie-Pott-case-Teen-sex-attackers-accused-writing-I-naked-
body-sexual-assault.html.

Davis, David Brion. 1988. *The Problem of Slavery in Western Culture*. Oxford: Oxford
University Press.

Delaney, Tim. 2008. *Shameful Behaviors*. Lanham, MD: University Press of America.

Denver Channel. 2014. "Frat Brothers Scrawled Slurs All Over CU Student's Body:
Gordie Bailey's Family Considers Suing." *Denver Channel*, October 8. http://
www.thedenverchannel.com/news/frat-brothers-scrawled-slurs-all-over-cu-
student-s-body.

Detel, Henne. 2013. "Disclosure and Public Shaming in the Age of Visibility." In
Media and Public Shaming: Drawing the Boundaries of Disclosure, edited by Julian
Petley, 77–96. New York: I. B. Taurus.

De Vries, Mary A. 2000. *The New American Handbook of Letter Writing*. 2nd ed.
Kolkata, India: Signet.

Dick, Kirby. 2012. *The Hunting Ground*. Documentary film. Available on Netflix.
Los Angeles: Weinstein Company.

Duffy, John. 2017. "The Good Writer: Virtue, Ethics, and the Teaching of Writing."
College English 79 (3): 229–50.

Dukes, Clement. 1893. "Work and Overwork in Relation to Health in Schools, an
Address Delivered before the Teacher's Guild of Great Britain and Ireland at Its
Fifth General Conference Held in Oxford on the 17th, 18th, 19th, and 20th of
April 1893." London: Percival.

Edge, Laura B. 2009. *Locked Up: A History of the U.S. Prison System*. Minneapolis:
Twenty-First Century Books.

Edwins, Laura. 2013. "Illinois Man Convicted in Noose Attack Ordered to Write
Essay on Lynching." *Christian Science Monitor*, February 28. http://www.
csmonitor.com/USA/Justice/2013/0228/Illinois-man-convicted-in-noose-attack-
ordered-to-write-essay-on-lynching.

Eisinger, Robert M. 2011. "The Political Non-Apology." *Social Science and Public
Policy* 48 (2): 136–41. https://doi.org/10.1007/s12115-010-9409-0.

Ellis v. Cleveland Municipal School District. 2006. No. 05-3192. US Court of
Appeals, Sixth Circuit. https://scholar.google.com/scholar_case?case=181319471
4321807319&q=%22name+on+the+board%22&hl=en&as_sdt=400006.

Ferrise, Adam. 2014. "Accused Bully Says Judge Who Sentenced Him to Hold Sign in Public 'Destroyed' His Life." Cleveland.com, April 13. http://www.cleveland.com/metro/index.ssf/2014/04/accused_bully_says_judge_who_s.html.

Fifth Estate Collective. 1977. "Fifth Estate #282." *Fifth Estate*, April–May. https://www.fifthestate.org/archive/282-april-may-1977/criticismself-criticism.

Foucault, Michel. 1977. *Discipline and Punish: The Birth of the Prison*. Translated by Alan Sheridan. New York: Pantheon Books.

Fox, Catherine Olive-Marie. 2014. "Toward a Queerly Classed Analysis of Shame: Attunement to Bodies in English Studies." *College English* 76 (4): 337–56.

Fraley, Malaika. 2012. "Federal Judge Requires Richmond Robbery Defendant to Submit Book Reports While Free on Bond." *Mercury News*, May 15. http://www.mercurynews.com/2012/05/15/federal-judge-requires-richmond-robbery-defendant-to-submit-book-reports-while-free-on-bond.

Freud, Sigmund. 1900. *The Interpretation of Dreams*. Translated by James Strachey. New York: Basic Books. http://psychclassics.yorku.ca/Freud/Dreams/dreams.pdf.

Friedersdorf, Conor. 2018. "The Excesses of Call-Out Culture." *Atlantic*, February 19. https://www.theatlantic.com/politics/archive/2018/02/what-good-can-come-of-callout-culture/553661.

Fuller, Bee. 2010. "Love, Jail and Jealousy: 'Dog' Tattoo Revenge Attacker Gets 14 Years." *Sidney Morning Herald*, December 10. http://www.smh.com.au/nsw/love-jail-and-jealousy-dog-tattoo-revenge-attacker-gets-14-years-20101209-18rtc.html.

Gardner, Trevor. 2016. *Discipline over Punishment: Successes and Struggles with Restorative Justice*. New York: Rowman and Littlefield.

Garfinkel, Harold. 1956. "Conditions of Successful Degradation Ceremonies." *American Journal of Sociology* 61 (5): 420–24.

Gayle, Damien. 2014. "Pimps Tattoo Their Names on Prostitutes' Bodies to Mark Their 'Property': Police Find Gang Marked Hookers As Sign of 'Loyalty.'" *Daily Mail*, October 16. http://www.dailymail.co.uk/news/article-2795610/pimps-tattoo-names-prostitutes-bodies-mark-property-police-gang-marked-sex-workers-sign-loyalty.html.

Gibson, Craig. 2014. "Better Living through Prose Composition? Moral and Compositional Pedagogy in Ancient Greek and Roman Progymnasmata." *Rhetorica: A Journal of the History of Rhetoric* 32 (1): 1–30.

Gilchriese, Sarah. 2015. "Organizational Discourse and Discursive Closure on College Sex Assaults: An Autoethnography about Filing a Title IX Complaint." Undergraduate honors thesis, University of Colorado, Boulder. http://scholar.colorado.edu/cgi/viewcontent.cgi?article=2006&context=honr_theses.

Goldman, Lauren. 2015. "Trending Now: The Use of Social Media Websites in Public Shaming Punishments." *American Criminal Law Review* 52:415–51.

Grise, Chrisanne. 2013. "Drug Dealer Is Ordered to Write 5,000 Word Essay." *Fix*, March 29. https://www.thefix.com/content/drug-dealer-sentenced-5000-word-essay91473.

Gruber, M. Catherine. 2014. *"I'm Sorry for What I've Done": The Language of Courtroom Apology.* Oxford: Oxford University Press.

Grunberger, Richard. 1995. *The 12-Year Reich: A Social History of Nazi Germany, 1933–1945.* Cambridge, MA: Da Capo Press.

Gump, Martin, v. William Walker Jr. 2005. Case No. 2004CA00367. Court of Appeals of Ohio, Fifth District, Stark County. https://scholar.google.com/scholar_case?case=2515828657357949613&q=%22wrote+on+his+body%22&hl=en&as_sdt=400006.

Gutowski, Christy, and Stacy St. Clair. 2017. "5 Wheaton College Football Players Face Felony Charges in Hazing Incident." *Chicago Tribune*, September 19. http://www.chicagotribune.com/news/local/breaking/ct-wheaton-college-football-hazing-met-20170918-story.html.

Hansen, Mark. 2013. "Woman Sentenced to Write an Essay on 'How a Lady Should Behave in Public.'" *ABA Journal*, July 11. http://www.abajournal.com/news/article/woman_sentenced_to_write_an_essay_on_behaving_like_a_lady_in_public.

Herzog, Katie. 2018. "Call-Out Culture Is a Toxic Garbage Dumpster Fire of Trash." *Stranger*, January 23. https://www.thestranger.com/slog/2018/01/23/25741141/call-out-culture-is-a-toxic-garbage-dumpster-fire-of-trash.

Hill, Frank. 2008. "Restorative Justice: Sketching a New Legal Discourse." *International Journal of Punishment and Sentencing* 4 (2): 51–81.

Hogan, Michael Phinney. 1985. "Writing as Punishment." *English Journal* 74 (5): 40–42.

Hollin, Clive R. 2013. *Psychology and Crime: An Introduction to Criminological Psychology.* 2nd ed. London: Routledge.

"How Not to Write an Apology." N.d. http://www.apologyletters.net/How_Not_To_Write_An_Apology.php.

"How to Write an Apology Letter." N.d. www.wikihow.com/Write-an-Apology-Letter.

"'I Like to Steal from Others and Lie about It': Parents Make Daughter, 8, Stand Outside School Wearing Humiliating Sign around her Neck." 2012. *Daily Mail*, April 18. http://www.dailymail.co.uk/news/article-2131709/Amiyah-White-Parents-make-daughter-8-stand-outside-school-wearing-I-like-steal-sign-neck.html.

Illinois General Assembly. 1973. "Crime Victims Compensation Act." 740 ILCS 45. http://www.ilga.gov/legislation/ilcs/ilcs3.asp?ActID=2028&ChapAct=740%A0ILCS%A045/&ChapterID=57&ChapterName=CIVIL+LIABILITIES&ActName=Crime+Victims+Compensation+Act.

International Labour Office. 2012. "ILO Global Estimate of Forced Labor." http://un-act.org/publication/view/ilo-global-estimate-forced-labour-2012.

Jacobs, Andrew. 2010. "China Pushes to End Public Shaming." *New York Times*, July 27. http://www.nytimes.com/2010/07/28/world/asia/28china.html.

Jauregui, Andres. 2013. "Chicago Teens Accused of Gang-Raping Girl, Posting

Video to Facebook, Will Be Tried As Adults." *Huffington Post*, May 19. http://www.huffingtonpost.com/2013/05/19/chicago-teens-gang-raping-girl-facebook_n_3303311.html.

Johnson, Shontavia. 2016. "Branded: Trademark Tattoos, Slave Owner Brands, and the Right to Have 'Free' Skin." *Michigan Telecommunications and Technology Law Review* 22 (2): 225–69.

"Judge Demands Biblical Book Report from Convicted Drunk Driver." 2012. RT. http://rt.com/usa/judge-demands-drunk-punishment-243.

"Judge's Sentence Involving Christian Book Causes Controversy." 2011. KHOU. http://www.khou.com/news/judges-sentence-involving-christian-book-causes-controversy/341212813.

Kador, John. 2009. *Effective Apology: Mending Fences, Building Bridges, and Restoring Trust*. Oakland: Berrett-Koehler.

Kahan, Dan M., and Eric A. Posner. 1999. "Shaming White-Collar Criminals: A Proposal for Reform of the Federal Sentencing Guidelines." *Journal of Law and Economics* 42, no. S1: 365–92.

Kamen, Deborah. 2013. "Chattel Slaves." In *Status in Classical Athens*, by Deborah Kamen. Princeton, NJ: Princeton University Press.

Kampf, Zohar. 2009. "Public (Non-)Apologies: The Discourse of Minimizing Responsibility." *Journal of Pragmatics* 41 (11): 2257–70.

Kannanl, Sindhu. 2012. "Cops Make Students Riding on Footboard Write Imposition." *Times of India*, December 20. http://timesofindia.indiatimes.com/city/chennai/Cops-make-students-riding-on-footboard-write-imposition/articleshow/17685532.cms.

Kant, Immanuel. 1796. *The Philosophy of Law: An Exposition of the Fundamental Principles of Jurisprudence as the Science of Right*. Pt. 2. Translated by William Hastie. http://oll.libertyfund.org/titles/kant-the-philosophy-of-law.

Kelly, Annie. 2014. "'I Carried His Name on My Body for Nine Years': The Tattooed Trafficking Survivors Reclaiming Their Past." *Guardian*, November 15. https://www.theguardian.com/global-development/2014/nov/16/sp-the-tattooed-trafficking-survivors-reclaiming-their-past.

Kenny, William. 2014. "Man Held Captive, Forcibly Tattooed in Mayfair Home." *Northeast Times*, April 9. http://www.northeasttimes.com/2014/apr/9/man-held-captive-forcibly-tattooed-mayfair-home.

Keyes, Ralph. 2010. *Euphemania: Our Love Affair with Euphemisms*. Boston: Little Brown.

Kirkland, David E. 2009. "The Skin We Ink: Tattoos, Literacy, and a New English Education." *English Education*, July, 375–95.

Klein, Kitty, and Adriel Boals. 2001. "Expressive Writing Can Increase Working Memory Capacity." *Journal of Experimental Psychology* 130 (1): 520–33.

Knoblauch, A. Abby. 2011. "A Textbook Argument: Definitions of Argument in Leading Composition Textbooks." *College Composition and Communication* 63 (2): 244–68.

Koeller, Austin. 2015. "Human Trafficking Nightmare." *Antelope*, April 15. http://unkantelope.com/wordpress_antelope/2015/04/15/human-trafficking-nightmare.

Koestenbaum, Wayne. 2011. *Humiliation*. New York: Picador.

Koritansky, Peter Karl. 2011. "The Problem of Punishment and the Return to the History of Political Thought." In *The Philosophy of Punishment and the History of Political Thought*, edited by Peter Karl Koritansky, 1–9. Columbia: University of Missouri Press.

Kristof, Nicholas. 2012. "She Has a Pimp's Name Etched on Her." *New York Times*, May 23. http://www.nytimes.com/2012/05/24/opinion/kristof-she-has-a-pimps-name-etched-on-her.html.

Kuruvilla, Carol. 2013. "Sick Miami Pimp Forces 13-Year-Old Runaway to Tattoo His Name on Her Eyelids: Eops." *New York Daily News*, March 30. http://www.nydailynews.com/news/crime/pimp-forces-teen-runaway-tattoo-eyelids-article-1.1303396.

La Ganga, Maria, and Kate Mather. 2013. "More Twists in the Audrie Pott Case." *Los Angeles Times*, April 15. http://articles.latimes.com/2013/apr/15/local/la-me-audrie-pott-20130416.

Laidlaw, Katherine. 2013. "High Times at Appleby College: Inside a Bitter Legal Dispute over Discipline at the Posh Private School." *Toronto Life*, July 24. http://torontolife.com/city/hight-times-at-appleby-collage.

Larsson, Stieg. 2008. *The Girl with the Dragon Tattoo*. New York: Alfred A. Knopf.

Lazare, Aaron. 2003. *On Apology*. Oxford: Oxford University Press.

Leibowitz, Glenn. 2016. "Why Every New Graduate Needs This Skill to Succeed—And 6 Ways to Learn It: Knowing How to Write Well Is a Skill Every New Graduate Needs to Succeed." *Inc.*, June 10. http://www.inc.com/glenn-leibowitz/why-every-new-graduate-needs-this-skill-to-succeed%E2%80%8A-%E2%80%8Aand-6-ways-to-learn-it.html.

Leong, Pamela. 2015. "American Graffiti: Deconstructing Gendered Communication Patterns in Bathroom Stalls." *Gender, Place, and Culture* 23 (3): 306–27.

Mandak, Joe. 2015. "Ex-Justice Joan Orie Melvin Disbarred by Consent Agreement." Philly.com. http://www.philly.com/philly/news/politics/20150116_ap_589a1d506b664d5b9570f77b4f09361c.html.

Matthäus, Jürgen, and Mark Roseman. 2010. *Jewish Responses to Persecution: 1933–1938*. Lanham, MD. Rowan and Littlefield.

Mayor, Adrienne. 1999. "People Illustrated: In Antiquity Tattoos Could Beautify, Shock, or Humiliate." *Archaeology*, March/April, 54–57.

McGough, Laura J. 2006. "Demons, Nature, or God? Witchcraft Accusations and the French Disease in Early Modern Venice." *Bulletin of the History of Medicine* 80 (2): 219–46.

Meisner, Jason. 2013. "Man Convicted in Noose Attack Ordered to Write Essay on Lychings." *Chicago Tribune*, February 28. http://articles.chicagotribune.

com/2013-02-28/news/ct-met-hate-crime-sentencing-20130228_1_lynchings-guilty-next-week-noose.

"Michael Bell, Jr., Kendall Seventh-Grader, Wears Sandwich Board on Street Corner As Punishment for Bad Grades." 2012. *Huffington Post*, March 12. http://www.huffingtonpost.com/2012/03/12/bad-grades-sandwich-board_n_1338938.html.

Miller, Joshua Rhett. 2011. "Houston Judge Stops Offering Convicts Choice of Christian Book Report or Community Service after Critics Blast Practice." FOX News, March 29. http://www.foxnews.com/us/2011/03/29/houston-judge-stops-christian-book-report-option-critics-blast-practice.

Milward, David. 2008. "Making the Circle Stronger: An Effort to Buttress Aboriginal Use of Restorative Justice in Canada against Recent Criticisms." *International Journal of Punishment and Sentencing* 4 (3): 124–58.

Mithal, Vibhav. 2004. "Whether the Doctrine of Informed Consent Is Rhetoric: Understanding Autonomy and Informed Consent in the Indian Context." *Asian Bioethics Review* 6 (1): 39–54.

"Mom Shames Cyber Bully Daughter by Posting Her Photo Holding an Apology Card on Facebook." 2014. News18, January 15. http://www.news18.com/news/buzz/mom-shames-cyber-bully-daughter-by-posting-her-photo-holding-an-apology-card-on-facebook-661964.html.

Morris, Phillip. 2012. "Woman Sentenced to Carry the 'Idiot' Sign Is Just the Tip of an Idiot Culture." Cleveland.com, November 14. http://www.cleveland.com/morris/index.ssf/2012/11/woman_sentenced_to_carry_the_i.html.

Mueller, Pam A., and Daniel M. Oppenheimer. 2014. "The Pen Is Mightier Than the Keyboard: Advantages of Longhand over Laptop Note Taking." *Psychological Science* 25 (6): 1159–68.

Murphy, Peter. 2013. "Reading Offers Brazilian Prisoners Quicker Escape." Reuters, June 25. http://www.reuters.com/article/2012/06/25/us-brazil-prison-reading-idUSBRE85O0WR20120625.

Murray, Gary V. 2007. "Perjurer Sentenced to Write Essay on 'Integrity.'" *Telegram*, March 31. http://www.telegram.com/article/20070331/NEWS/703310341/1008.

Music Intern. 2015. "BBC—Human Trafficking Interview with Jennifer Kempton." WCBE, August 24. http://wcbe.org/post/bbc-human-trafficking-interview-jennifer-kempton.

Nazaryan, Alexander. 2012. "Write a Book Report, Avoid Jail: Judge Orders Man Freed If He Commits to Literature." *Daily News*, May 16. http://www.nydailynews.com/blogs/pageviews/write-book-report-avoid-jail-judge-orders-man-freed-commits-literature-blog-entry-1.1638322.

NCTE (National Council of Teachers of English). 1984. "Resolution on Condemning the Use of Writing as Punishment." http://www.ncte.org/positions/statements/writingaspunishment.

New Hampshire Legislature. 2014. "Relative to Trafficking In Persons." NH SB317. https://legiscan.com/NH/text/SB317/id/1040746.

Nussbaum, Martha C. 2004. "Shaming Citizens?" In *Hiding from Humanity*, edited by Martha Nussbaum, 222–79. Princeton, NJ: Princeton University Press.

Ong, Walter J. 1982. *Orality and Literacy: The Technologizing of the Word.* London: Routledge.

Oppel, Robert. 2013. "Ohio Teenagers Guilty in Rape That Social Media Brought to Light." *New York Times*, March 17. http://www.nytimes.com/2013/03/18/us/teenagers-found-guilty-in-rape-in-steubenville-ohio.html?_r=0.

Ovalle, David. 2015. "Former Gulliver Swimmer Gets Probation in Sex-Video Case." *Miami Herald*, January 15. http://www.miamiherald.com/news/local/crime/article6726045.html.

Owen, Glen. 2014. "Gove Orders Return to Old-Fashioned School Discipline—with Pupils 'Writing Lines.'" *Daily Mail*, February 1. http://www.dailymail.co.uk/news/article-2550265/Gove-orders-return-old-fashioned-school-discipline-pupils-writing-lines.html.

Pederson, Terri. 2015. "Hartford Woman Gets 360 Days Jail, $340,000 Restitution to Vet Clinic She Embezzled From." *Beaver Dam Daily Citizen*, January 22. http://host.madison.com/news/local/crime_and_courts/hartford-woman-gets-days-jail-restitution-to-vet-clinic-she/article_809db9fd-e336-58ba-9ef7-cdcc598be8e4.html.

Pennell, Elizabeth Robins. 1887. "Harrow-on-the-Hill." *St. Nicholas* 14 (6): 404–12. http://ufdc.ufl.edu/UF00065513/00183/10j?search=writing+is+the+penance.

People v. Dale J. Jung. 1999. Court of Appeal, Second District, Division 5, California, No. B114721.

People v. Jerron Callahan. 2009. 2d Crim. No. B205001. Court of Appeals of California, Second Appellate District, Division Six.

Pew Research Center. 2008. "Tattooed Gen Nexters." http://www.pewresearch.org/fact-tank/2008/12/09/tattooed-gen-nexters.

Pritchard, Connor, and Dominic Russo. 2010. *The Party Bible: The Good Book for Great Times.* Avon, MA: Adams Media.

Rawlings, Dillon. 2016. "Sacred Heart School Turns 125." *Benito Link*, August 25. http://benitolink.com/sacred-heart-school-turns-125.

Read, Tracey. 2013. "Girl Says Bullying at Mentor School Drove Her to Bomb Threat." *News-Herald*, June 5. http://www.news-herald.com/general-news/20130605/girl-says-bullying-at-mentor-school-drove-her-to-bomb-threat.

Robert Lee Menyweather v. State of Texas. 2014. Case No. 05-13-01108-CR. Court of Appeals, Fifth District of Texas at Dallas

Rodogno, Raffaele. 2009. "Shame, Guilt, and Punishment." *Law and Philosophy* 28 (5): 429–64.

Romanes, George J. 1879. "The Science and Philosophy of Recreation." *Popular Science Monthly*, October, 789.

Ronson, Jon. 2015. *So You've Been Publicly Shamed.* New York: Riverhead.

Rose, Shirley K. 1990. "Reading Representative Anecdotes of Literacy Practice; or 'See Dick and Jane Read and Write!'" *Rhetoric Review* 8 (2): 244–59.

Rosenthal, George. N.d. "Auschwitz-Birkenau: The Evolution of Tattooing in the

Auschwitz Concentration Camp Complex." *Jewish Virtual Library*. http://www.jewishvirtuallibrary.org/jsource/Holocaust/tattoos1.html.

Ross, Tenley. 2015. "Bradford County Offers Public Shaming as Probation Condition." WUFT, March 17. http://www.wuft.org/news/2015/03/17/bradford-county-offers-public-shaming-as-probation-condition.

Rubin v. Lafayette Parish School Board. 1995. "Bernadette Rubin, Plaintiff-Appellant, v. Lafayette Parish School Board, Defendant-Appellee." Court of Appeal of Louisiana, Third Circuit. March 1.

Ruta, Brandon, dir. 2014. *Branded: Sex Slavery in America*. CNN Freedom Project: Ending Modern-Day Slavery. Written by Haley Press and Brandon Ruta. Documentary film. 26 minutes. http://www.cnn.com/videos/world/2015/09/14/spc-freedom-project-sex-slavery-in-america.cnn/video/playlists/cnn-freedom-project-human-trafficking.

Salonga, Robert. 2013. "Audrie Pott Case: Documents Detail Party, Acts at Heart of Sexual Assault Blamed for Teen's Suicide." *Mercury News*, April 15. http://www.mercurynews.com/ci_23029884/audrie-pott-case-documents-detail-party-at-heart.

Sedgwick, Eve Kosofsky, and Adam Frank. 1995a. *Shame and Its Sisters: A Silvan Tomkins Reader*. Durham, NC: Duke University Press.

———. 1995b. "Shame in the Cybernetic Fold: Reading Silvan Tomkins." *Critical Inquiry* 21 (2): 496–522.

Seymour, Anne, Sharon English, and Jill Weston. 2001. "Offender Apologies." Washington, DC: Justice Solutions. http://www.justicesolutions.org/art_pub_offender_apologies.htm.

Shalhoup, Dean. 2015. "Plea Deal Gives Nashua Domestic Violence Offender Chance 'To Totally Change His Life.'" *Nashua Telegraph*, January 26. http://www.nashuatelegraph.com/news/1056031-469/plea-deal-gives-nashua-domestic-violence-offender.html.

Sharma, Amita. 2011. "Pimps Recruiting Underage Girls in San Diego through Force and Coercion." KPBS, October 31. http://www.kpbs.org/news/2011/oct/31/pimps-recruiting-underage-girls-san-diego-county-t.

Simonds, Lauren. 2013. "Good Writing Can Help You Succeed." *Time*, April 19. http://business.time.com/2013/04/19/good-writing-can-help-you-succeed.

Simpson, Mark. 2008. "Assume the Position: A Queer Defense of Hazing." *Out Magazine*, August 10. http://www.out.com/entertainment/2006/08/10/assume-position.

Smith, Richard. 2013. "Drug Dealer Is Sentenced to Write a 5,000 Essay." *Mirror*, March 27. http://www.mirror.co.uk/news/uk-news/drug-dealer-sentenced-write-essay-1787006.

Smith, Stephen. 2007. "Dead Frat Pledge's Body Defaced." CBS News, January 10. http://www.cbsnews.com/news/dead-frat-pledges-body-defaced.

Soares, Lina Bell, and Karen Wood. 2010. "A Critical Literacy Perspective for Teaching and Learning Social Studies." *Reading Teacher* 63 (6): 486–94.

Sofie Karasek v. Regents of the University of California. 2015. Case No. 15-cv-03717-WHO. US District Court, N.D. California.

Spillett, Richard. 2014. "Schoolgirl, 12, Is Ordered to Write 'Decent People Take Pride in Their Appearance' 40 Times and Then Sent Home—for Wearing the Wrong Shoes." *Daily Mail*, September 9. http://www.dailymail.co.uk/news /article-2749511/Decent-people-pride-appearance-Schoolgirl-12-ordered-lines-sent-home-wearing-wrong-shoes.html.

Stewart, Gail B. 2014. *A Cultural History of Tattoos*. San Diego: Reference Point Press.

Sweeney, Annie. 2012. "Convicted Pimp Sentenced to Life in Prison." *Chicago Tribune*, November 26. http://articles.chicagotribune.com/2012-11-26/news/ ct-met-human-trafficking-sentence-20121127_1_massage-parlors-life-sentence-illegal-immigrants.

Taft, Lee. 2000. "Apology Subverted: The Commodification of Apology." *Yale Law Journal* 109: 1135–60.

Taft, Victoria. 2015. "Judge Gets Crafty with Sentence, Gives Attacker 2 Options: Go to Jail or Relive Crime as the Victim." *Independent Journal Review*. http://ijr.com/2015/05/332762-judge-gave-option-punishment-fit-crime-took-right-face.

Tan, Alicia. 2016. "Students Late for Class Forced to Write 1,000 Emojis for Punishment." *Mashable*, April 22. http://mashable.com/2016/04/22/emoji-punishment /#OHiDGAebq5qx.

Taylor, Beverly. 2015. "'Scarred by the Sex Trade': Tattoo Artist Helping Victims Break Free from Their 'Brands' and Their Pimps." Fox6Now, February 8. http://fox6now.com/2015/02/08/scarred-by-the-sex-trade-a-closer-look-into-the-underworld-of-sex-trafficking.

"Teen Forced to Hold 'I Steal from My Family' Sign on Street Corner As Punishment." 2012. *Huffington Post*, February 15. http://www.huffingtonpost.com/2012/02/15/teen-forced-to-hold-i-steal-from-my-family-sign_n_1278946.html.

Tyre, Peg. 2012. "The Writing Revolution." *Atlantic*, October. https://www.theatlantic.com/magazine/archive/2012/10/the-writing-revolution/309090.

UK Department for Education. 2016. "Behaviour and Discipline in Schools: Advice for Headteachers and School Staff." https://www.gov.uk/government/uploads/ system/uploads/attachment_data/file/488034/Behaviour_and_Discipline_in_Schools_-_A_guide_for_headteachers_and_School_Staff.pdf.

United States v. Alex A. Campbell. 2014. Case No. 12-3724. US Court of Appeals, Seventh Circuit.

United States v. Gementera. 2004. Case No. 03-10103. US Court of Appeals, Ninth Circuit.

US Code. 2011. "Trademarks: General Provisions." In *Commerce and Trade*. Washington, DC: US Government Printing Office. https://www.gpo.gov/fdsys/pkg/ USCODE-2011-title15/html/USCODE-2011-title15-chap22-subchapIII-sec1127.htm.

US Department of State. N.d. "What Is Modern Slavery?" https://www.state.gov/j/tip/what.

US Holocaust Memorial Museum. N.d. "The Boycott of Jewish Businesses." Holocaust Encyclopedia. https://www.ushmm.org/outreach/en/article.php?ModuleId=10007693.

———. N.d. "Tattoos and Numbers: The System of Identifying Prisoners at Auschwitz." Holocaust Encyclopedia. https://www.ushmm.org/wlc/en/article.php?ModuleId=10007056.

Valiente, Alexa. 2015. "Why an Ohio Judge Is Using Unusual Punishments to Keep People out of Jail." ABC News, September 1. http://abcnews.go.com/US/ohio-judge-unusual-punishments-people-jail/story?id=33440871.

Vandervort, Lucinda. 2013. "Sexual Consent as Voluntary Agreement: Tales of 'Seduction' or Questions of Law?" *New Criminal Law Review* 16 (1): 143–201.

Van Ness, Daniel W., and Karen Heetderks Strong. 2014. *Restoring Justice: An Introduction to Restorative Justice.* 5th ed. Abingdon, UK: Taylor and Francis.

Walker-Rodriguez, Amanda, and Rodney Hill. 2011. "Human Sex Trafficking." FBI Law Enforcement Bulletin. https://leb.fbi.gov/2011/march/human-sex-trafficking.

Walsh, Jeremy. 2011. "Investigators Testify." *Record-Bee Community News*, February 10. http://www.record-bee.com/general-news/20110210/investigators-testify.

Wan, Amy J. 2011. "In the Name of Citizenship: The Writing Classroom and the Promise of Citizenship." *College English* 74 (1): 28–49.

Weyeneth, Robert R. 2001. "The Power of Apology and the Process of Historical Reconciliation." *Public Historian* 23 (3): 9–38.

Wipper, Audrey. 1988. "Reflections on the Past Sixteen Years, 1972–1988, and Future Challenges." *Canadian Journal of African Studies / Revue Canadienne Des Études* 22:3. 409–21.

"Woman Sentenced to Write Apology Letter to City." 2014. KLTV. http://www.kltv.com/story/25468933/woman-sentenced-to-write-apology-letter-to-city.

Workman, Thomas. 2001. "Finding the Meanings of College Drinking: An Analysis of Fraternity Drinking Stories." *Health Communication* 13 (4): 427–47. http://digitalcommons.unl.edu/commstudiespapers/3.

INDEX

Page numbers in italics refer to figures.